Awakening Your Spiritual Life

A collection of short inspirational Bible studies and teachings to encourage and enhance your relationship with the Lord

LEX ADAMS

WESTBOW
PRESS®
A DIVISION OF THOMAS NELSON
& ZONDERVAN

WestBow Press books may be ordered through booksellers or by contacting:

WestBow Press
A Division of Thomas Nelson & Zondervan
1663 Liberty Drive
Bloomington, IN 47403
www.westbowpress.com
844-714-3454

Scripture taken from the King James Version of the Bible.

ISBN: 978-1-6642-5442-8 (sc)
ISBN: 978-1-6642-5441-1 (hc)
ISBN: 978-1-6642-5443-5 (e)

Library of Congress Control Number: 2022901472

Print information available on the last page.

WestBow Press rev. date: 01/26/2022

Dedicated to the Lord Jesus Christ and the souls for whom He died; that man might have fellowship with God the Father.

Introduction

One of the most crucial needs in our day is for the Christian to learn to focus on Jesus - to trust in the word of God and the inner working of God's Spirit amidst the many influences which attempt to hinder his relationship with God.

This book is written with the prayer that the contents will help to firmly establish the believer upon a proper and solid foundation in Christ. Paul warns against building upon the foundation of faith in Jesus with things which are not of God's Spirit, as we read in 1 Corinthians 3:10-15, "But let every man take heed how he buildeth thereupon. For other foundation can no man lay than that is laid, which is Jesus Christ. Now if any man build upon this foundation gold, silver, precious stones, wood, hay, stubble; every man's work shall be made manifest: for the day shall declare it, because it shall be revealed by fire; and the fire shall try every man's work of what sort it is. If any man's work abide which he hath built thereupon, he shall receive a reward. If any man's work shall be burned, he shall suffer loss: but he himself shall be saved; yet so as by fire." For this reason, it is important to lay the first building blocks in the Spirit properly to avoid later destruction or loss.

This book is a compilation of periodical writings with each chapter standing alone as a meditative look at various portions of the Bible. Each chapter can be considered a Bible study or devotional to be read slowly and prayerfully. With chapters addressing encouragement for the heart, faith, Christian maturity, and yielding to the Lord, the book touches on many different needs for the believer today. To receive the maximum benefit from each portion, allow time to prayerfully consider the message with your Bible with you and take the time to look up and read the scriptures referenced. Allow God to quicken His truth in your heart. The Holy Spirit is the teacher, and as your eyes are upon Him, He will surely enlighten and minister far beyond the printed page. I recommend reading the chapters separately, over time, rather than at one sitting. Some of the material is deep and weighty. So, as you read, ask God to give you a teachable spirit, to be able to receive from Him the light of His word.

The cross is not only a Christian symbol in remembrance of Jesus, but is also a spiritual principle, that the Holy Spirit desires to apply to our hearts. It is a central theme in the Gospel message. Our own hearts can shade our perception of God and His truth when sullied with our own thinking and prejudice. As a prism deflects and changes light, so our hearts interpret God to the level of our understanding. We see Him more clearly through the loving and persistent work of the Holy Spirit in our hearts, as we understand the principle of the cross. The treasures of truth reflect more beautifully and accurately through us as we yield to His Spirit. It was through Jesus's crucifixion and death that He experienced the resurrection. His resurrection power and light transform our lives, as we submit to the precious work of the cross in our hearts.

The biblical promise of blessing and joy to God's people is repeated throughout scripture. The Bible speaks of complete joy, abundance in blessings, healing, deliverance, protection, comfort, peace, and every other possible good thing one could ever desire. And it speaks of it in terms of experiencing it today, not only when we get to heaven. Our difficulty is learning how to receive His blessings, and to listen to His voice of instruction and guidance. We easily miss the path because of a lack of understanding, which if we had, would cause us to be overtaken by His blessings and goodness. The secret is not in seeking the blessings, but in learning to yield the inner self-will to God and allowing God to accomplish His inner work of transformation in our hearts.

Life is often difficult. As Christians, we can become discouraged, confused, and feel shackled by the many things that touch our lives, which for a time we may not understand. These very things are often the doors through which God would bring us into His life of blessing. God's most abundant blessings are for those who learn to think as Jesus would, in every situation of life, beyond our time in church, worship, and Christian service. This book is written to help the believer make sense out of the many difficulties and testing that come our way, and to allow God to use them to bring us into His purposes, blessing, and peace. scripture is rich with words of encouragement, examples of the struggles and victories of others, and God's insight into everything that may touch our lives.

Seeing the answers is not always easy. It is our prayer that these chapters may help you find a greater peace, a deeper joy, and a fresh comfort in the circumstances in which you find yourself. This is possible as we seek to learn what the Holy Spirit is trying to teach us in each situation. God's goal is for us to mature into the likeness of Jesus, to have inner peace and joy, and to glorify His name. Our challenge is to learn how to cooperate with the Holy Spirit, to seek to be teachable, and to yield our hindering self-life to Him. As we learn these lessons, we also are granted the privilege of receiving and enjoying some of our inheritance here, today!

May the Holy Spirit minister, as only He can, to the needs of your heart through the teachings in this book.

And Jesus Stood Still and Commanded Him to Be Called

Mark 10:49

Heavenly Father, once again we come to You bringing every care and concern. We are privileged that through the name of Jesus we are granted an audience at the very highest throne of all power and authority. This is amazing to us, as we realize that He, who created all things, has committed to listen to our petitions because we approach Your throne in the name of Your Son, Jesus. Thank You for Your great compassion toward us. Praise be unto You, for You are a glorious God. Let us learn to worship You in the beauty of holiness, for our relationship with You is a sacred thing to be cherished. In Jesus's name we pray. Amen.

Faith is a marvelous and mysterious thing. How it works and how it connects us with God is unexplainable. Somehow, something within the heart of man becomes alive, quickened by the Holy Spirit of God. Faith is not a frame of mind. It is a reality of the heart given by God to those who believe. The most beautiful thing about faith is how God reacts to it and receives it. Faith definitely connects the heart of the believer with the power of God, and the results are something very special.

People with quickened Holy Ghost faith are compelled into action. Four men, who knew a severely crippled man, had heard that Jesus was in a home in their city. They purposed to take their friend to Him. They carried him across town on a stretcher to the location of Jesus. Upon arriving at the home, the crowd was so great that they could not get him inside. However, this thing called faith pressed them forward. They had to get the crippled man to Jesus. So, they proceeded to tear apart the roof of the house. Once a hole was made, they lowered their friend into the home near Jesus. Faith had overpowered them. They knew that they must get this man to Jesus. They refused to be turned away by the crowd. A short time later, this man was walking home praising God for His mercy and healing. We read that when Jesus saw their faith he began to minister to the man, first proclaiming that his sins were forgiven and next causing him to walk. This is the wonderful response of God to true Holy Spirit faith. (Mark 2:1-12)

In Matthew 15 we read an extraordinary story of a woman's faith. She was not a Jew, not one unto whom Jesus was at this time sent to minister. But she had heard of Him. She believed in Him, and she came to Him. She asked Him to deliver her daughter from a devil. Jesus did not answer at first, but was silent. She persisted in her plea until the disciples of Jesus came and asked Him to send her away because of her annoying crying. He then explained that He was not sent to minister except to the children of Israel. When she heard this, she refused to accept His answer. Bowing at His feet, she continued to worship Him and requested His help. He however, again responded that it was not proper for Him to take that which was purposed for the children of Israel and give it unto dogs. Quite a humiliating statement to the woman. Perhaps she thought of herself as worthy in a wrong way and this was Jesus's way of humbling her. God only knows what He was working in this woman's heart, but in the face of this comment she yet persisted and stated, "Truth

Lord, yet the dogs eat of the crumbs which fall from their masters' table." (Matt. 15:27) She pleaded, "Master, yes, though I be only a dog in comparison to Israel, yet I plead with Thee for but a crumb from Thy table... just one crumb." Jesus, at this, could not resist her faith. He could not turn away. He would not turn away! He looked at this woman, saw her persistent faith and said to her, "O woman, great is thy faith: be it unto thee even as thou wilt." (Matt. 15:28) Faith was so alive in this woman that she could not turn away from seeking Jesus. It consumed her...it propelled her...it humbled her... it connected her with God, and she had to continue until she heard from Him. This is true Holy Ghost faith.

Bartimaeus was a blind man who would sit along the road outside the city of Jericho and beg for a living. He had heard about Jesus. One day, as he was sitting by the road, there was a commotion as a great many people began passing by that way. Bartimaeus was blind, but he could hear well, and he heard that it was Jesus who passed his way with many people following Him. Realizing in his heart that Jesus could heal his eyes, and knowing it beyond any shadow of a doubt, he began to cry aloud: "Jesus, thou son of David, have mercy on me." (Mark 10:47) Many around him, more than one, admonished him to "be quiet beggar... hold your peace." But something was alive in this man. Something more powerful than himself. A hope had been quickened at the hearing of the nearness of Jesus, and he began to cry aloud all the more. "Jesus, thou son of David, have mercy on me." (Mark 10:47) In the middle of the crowd Jesus stopped and stood still. Whether he heard Bartimaeus with His natural ears, or whether He heard the calling of faith, I do not know. We do know that Jesus stood still. He would go no farther. He had heard a call of faith from the heart of Bartimaeus. Jesus commanded that Bartimaeus be brought to Him, and asked him what he wanted from the Lord. Moments later Bartimaeus, with sight fully restored, was one of the multitudes that proceeded out of Jericho, following Jesus. (Mark 10:46-52)

The scripture is full of many more stories of faith alive and vibrant in the hearts of humans who were so moved and focused on the Lord that they would not be turned away until they had touched Him. In Mark 5 a ruler of the synagogue came to Him and a common woman with an issue of blood was healed. The picture is clear, Jesus responded to faith. Whether faith was in the ruler of the synagogue, a Gentile woman, a poor blind beggar, a soldier or a priest, Jesus would not pass them by. When He heard the call of faith, He stopped, stood still and took the time to minister to each one. He was drawn to faith... true, active, Holy Ghost, and heart-level faith. It didn't matter what the status of the person was for where faith was active, Jesus was there. He is no respecter of persons.

Lord, grant unto each one who needs Your help, for whatever reason, a quickening of faith to receive from Your gracious and compassionate hand that for which he prays. Let us see through faith that the throne to which we come is that of the Almighty. There is nothing, absolutely nothing, that is too hard for You or impossible with God. Let this be the foundation for all our prayers and our approach to all of life's challenges. Precious Jesus, it is in Your name we pray. Amen.

Thou God Seest Me

Gen. 16:13

Heavenly Father, we know that You take notice of even the smallest things in our lives and care about each of them. We thank You that You are never too busy to listen to our prayers; never too far away from us to draw near when we call upon You; never too superior to be burdened with our needs. Your willingness to be involved with us is a testimony of Your greatness and of Your great love for us. Thank You for Your caring and watchful eye which seeks to preserve us from darkness and turn each challenge into an opportunity to know more of You. We praise You and bow before You with grateful hearts. In Jesus's name we pray. Amen.

In our affliction, trials, seeking of God, times of blessing and the common activities of life, we can be assured that God sees us and beholds our situation. We can take encouragement from scripture and the testimonies of others that even when it seems things are too much to bear, God is near and ready to help.

In Genesis 16, Hagar was mistreated by Sarai. So bad was the treatment that Hagar ran away into the wilderness. She sought to escape a very difficult situation. Lo and behold, no sooner had she fled than an angel of the Lord met her and communed with her. He asked her, "Whence camest thou, and whither wilt thou go?" (Genesis 16:8) She explained her flight, but did not answer where she would go. It is not told us in scripture, but we assume that she had not thought of where she would go, but had only thought of the immediate desire to flee. This reaction is not uncommon when pressures of trials and adversity touch our lives. We often think to flee with little or no thought of the consequences or of where we will go. The words spoken to Hagar let her know that God had heard her affliction. That, in itself, was a great relief and comfort. (From this knowledge alone, we can gather much strength. God knows of my affliction! I am not without Him in this situation! This is refreshing for the soul.) The angel then told Hagar to return to Sarai and submit to her. There was more to be accomplished in this situation and Hagar was to be a part of what was developing. With the strength and comfort of knowing that God had seen her affliction, she returned.

In Acts chapter 8, we read of a high-ranking Ethiopian official of great authority (having served under Candace, the queen of Ethiopia) who was returning from Jerusalem. He had gone there to worship. He had taken a long journey from Ethiopia for the sole purpose of worshipping God. He was a seeker of God, and was now returning to his home and was reading the book of Isaiah (Esaias) in his chariot. God had seen this man. He had watched as he left Ethiopia to come to worship. God saw his spiritual hunger and was *very* aware of this one lone person traveling in the desert. God spoke to Philip and commanded him to go out into the desert as you go from Jerusalem to Gaza. And so, Philip went. He saw the Ethiopian's chariot and the Lord impressed upon Philip to go up to the chariot. As he approached, he heard the man reading the book of Isaiah aloud. As Philip and the Ethiopian spoke about Isaiah's words, the Ethiopian opened his heart to the message of the Lord Jesus, received Christ as his Savior, and was baptized. This Ethiopian returned home a new creature in Christ and rejoicing in how God had met him and revealed Himself unto him. God beheld this one lone individual and his desire for God, and God did not fail to reach out and touch him.

In Acts chapter 10 we read of a Roman soldier, a centurion or captain over 100 soldiers. This soldier endeavored to live a life seeking God. We are told that he prayed always and gave assistance to many people. Here he was, living his life as a soldier in the Roman army, praying and doing good to help those around him. Unknown to him, God had been keeping a record of this man Cornelius. God knew of all his prayers and of all his giving. One day in a vision God tells Cornelius, "Thy prayers and thine alms are come up for a memorial before God." (Acts 10:4) Something as simple as regular prayers and giving had come to be a memorial before God. God had seen this man. God had not ignored his dedication but had kept a record of it! Peter is then sent to Cornelius' house and as he is speaking about Jesus, the entire group is filled with the Holy Spirit. Salvation and the baptism of the Holy Spirit had come to Cornelius' home because of his seeking of God.

These are tremendous stories of God's watchful and caring eye overseeing each one who seeks Him. Whether in adversity, or in the routine of daily life, God does see. God does care, and He does draw near to those who suffer and who seek Him diligently. There was nothing fancy about Cornelius' life or walk with God. There was nothing spectacular about the Ethiopian's seeking of God. There was only a true desire and hunger for Him, and God moved to meet that hunger. His love reaches out to the one... to the individual... to you and to me.

Thank You, Lord, for Your tender and caring love for us and for Your ever-present help. Nothing touches us of which You are not aware, and nothing can harm us, for You are with us in all of life's experiences. In Jesus's name we pray. Amen.

Finding Inner Peace and Joy

Heavenly Father, we come to seek a greater ability and strength to quickly obey the promptings of Your Spirit in our lives. Make us sensitive to Your touch and the whisper of Your guidance. Cause us to yield our self-will to Thee and learn to exercise the power of our will to choose Your ways, as You make them clear to our hearts. Oh, Father, it is only in obedience that we find joy and clarity of understanding. Give us strength to obey in the face of our weakness. In Jesus's name we pray. Amen.

On Earth Peace, Good Will Toward Men (Luke 2:14)

At the birth of Jesus, shepherds in the field were visited by an angel and overshadowed by the glory of God. The angel told them of the birth of Jesus, the Savior, Christ the Lord. Then suddenly there was a whole host of angels praising God and saying, "glory to God in the highest, and on earth peace, good will toward men." (Luke 2:13-14) One angel came to give the message of "good tidings of great joy, which shall be to all people," (Luke 2:10) but the excitement of the message was such that a great number of other angels burst upon the scene praising God. This was history changing news being given to these shepherds. The spiritual beings of heaven understood the magnitude of what was taking place. This was the main event for all of history. There was overflowing excitement in Heaven over Jesus's coming and His purpose.

Often, we may find ourselves saying, "well, that's just wonderful that the angels are all excited, but I'm down here struggling through life, and I don't feel all that excited or blessed about anything. That is a nice message, peace, and good will and all, but I don't feel it. I don't have this peace. I don't feel excited about my faith and my walk with Jesus." The angels said it was a message of great joy! We may feel like, "great, but where is it? It somehow got lost between the manger and me in my life." Why does the joy escape us? Why is peace elusive all too often?

One thing is sure, peace and joy are here, and they are for every believer in Jesus. We know this because it is promised in the Bible. That being the case, we can then seek understanding about how to find this peace and joy and live a life full of them. Problems and challenges touch each of us. They are real, and they hurt and stretch us. We feel the pressure of many different circumstances and we watch as it seems one after the other presses against our lives. Jesus told us, in John 15:11, "These things have I spoken unto you, that my joy might remain in you, and that your joy might be full." The Lord's joy came from His inner desire and delight in doing the will of the Father. Psalm 40:8 reads of Jesus, "I delight to do thy will, 0 my God." This is part of the key to walking in peace and joy, learning to delight in doing God's will. We should not seek to do works to please God, but inwardly in the heart and mind learn to obey God. Works follow!

What things did Jesus say to us so that His joy would be in us, and our own joy full? In the first ten verses of the fifteenth chapter of John, Jesus gives several clear instructions to finding joy. Abide in Him and allow Him to abide in us. This sounds simple enough, but how does it work? It means choosing, when we are pressured to respond to a matter wrongly and in self-will, to listen to His inner voice and obey Him, not yielding to the voices of the flesh and the devil. Stay put in the Spirit. Don't fall into the lower nature response of wrong for wrong. If we are hurt, forgive, do not speak evil in return. If we are taken from, forgive, do not take back. If we are mistreated wrongfully and unfairly, suffer it, do not seek to get even.

These are not easy responses to deliver. Our nature fights such yielding. However, it is in learning to react like Jesus did that we will open the doors of peace and joy, although the doors may seem very heavy to push open at times. 1 Peter 2:19-23 sets forth the example of Christ in suffering and responding in a manner pleasing to God. We are called to the same response. We are called to respond in all things as Jesus did. This is not possible unless we are yielding to the Holy Spirit and the light of God's word in our moments of testing. As odd as it may seem, the challenges and pressures that come are brought so we may learn to enter in the joy of the Lord.

The doors on the palace of joy and peace are titled by many names which seem strange to our natural mind. One door reads, "Suffering wrongfully and not reacting." Another reads, "Being spoken evil of when it is not true and loving and forgiving the person who said it." Yet another reads, "Pray for those who despitefully use you." And another states, "Do good to them that hate you." And one reads, "Love ye your enemies." (Matt. 5:44; Luke 6:27-36) Why? So that bitterness and resentment cannot get a root hold on our hearts and cut us off from the joy of God. We do not need to pray that people continue to mistreat us, but we can pray that God would become real in the lives of those who appear, at the moment, to be our enemy. After all, Jesus died for them too! That is a thought we would like to avoid when we are smarting from the mistreatment of another. But Jesus loved them, forgave them, prayed "Father forgive them for they know not what they do," (Luke 23:24) and we are called to do the same. We are to obey the commandments of God. To do this we must be filled with the word of God and obey what we learn. If we hold anything more precious than pleasing God, we will find testing coming in that area. Our possessions, our employment, our family, our wants and dreams, our self-efforts, must one by one be brought into subjection to God before we can find peace and joy.

If we hold onto them, placing more importance on maintaining them than on obeying the Lord, we forfeit peace and joy. In fact, it is our fear and concern over losing things or position in life or relationships that causes us to forfeit peace and joy. It is in giving all things into His hands, and letting go, that we find true inner peace. Thy will be done Lord.

If we are born again and heaven bound, then everything that happens to us between now and heaven is for our good. Everything! We need to believe this and act like God knows what He is doing with our lives. Romans 8:28 states, "And we know that all things work together for good to them that love God, to them who are the called according to his purpose." And what is that purpose? It is stated in the next verse, "For whom he did foreknow, he also did predestinate to be conformed to the image of his Son." (Romans 8:29) This conforming to the image of Jesus is the result of the pressures and challenges that refine our responses until we learn to respond in all things as Jesus would.

Satan wants to rob the Christian of joy. He does this by attempting to cause us to look at the testing, look at the problems, and focus on them rather than on the inner work of the Holy Spirit. As we learn to welcome challenges and problems as God's refining hand, we defeat the devil and enter the joy of the Lord in the midst of our sometimes-unpleasant circumstances. Our joy does not come by God changing our circumstances or changing the people in our life we find difficult. That is Satan's lie. It is the evil one who attempts to get us into a mindset of, "if I only had this or that I would have joy." Or "if this thing or that thing in my life would just change or go away, then I would have joy and peace." These things are simply not true. Joy does not come from the changing of outward matters, but from inner light of God's word and learning to respond like Jesus.

We need to say in the face of all difficulties, "I am a blood-washed saint of God, I am heaven bound, God is in control of my life, and I will stand in my faith in Him in the midst of my current circumstances, whether they change or not, for my joy is to do the will of my Father." (See Hab.3: 17-19.) Then we can stand ready to receive the joy and blessing of God! Don't entertain Satan's bait that things and outward change bring joy. This is the lie the world is chasing after and it bears no spiritual fruit. God is always looking at how we react in situations. The situations themselves are only tools in God's hands. When we have mastered an inner issue, the situation will change to take us to the next level. We should not expect our refining to be over so soon. There is yet a lot of work for God to accomplish in each of us.

If we blame circumstances for our unhappiness, we have listened to the devil. Our unhappiness is most often a result of disobedience to God. (Though we experience sorrow and grief, we need not forfeit inner peace and joy.) Somewhere we have not yielded to His will. Somewhere we have taken matters into our own hands, to do our own will, to protect ourselves, or accomplish our own desires apart from Him. It is never our circumstance that is our problem, it is our inner attitude toward our circumstance. It is not other people that rob us of joy, it is Satan, as we listen to the flesh and self-will rather than the Holy Spirit. In the garden, Eve blamed the serpent for beguiling her. Adam blamed Eve for giving him the fruit. God held each of them responsible for their own sins. Satan may be the one beguiling us to look at our circumstances and think that by changing them, or other people, we would be happy; but it is our individual responsibility to resist his lies and obey God anyway. We have no one to blame for a lack of peace and joy but ourselves. If we obey God, we will be blessed, and that is certain. There is nothing that can take our joy or peace when we have entered there through the door of obedience.

If we join the devil and the flesh with "poor me, nothing ever goes right for me" type thinking, then we rob ourselves of God's blessing. We need to do what scripture says, "Be anxious for nothing, but in everything by prayer and supplication with thanksgiving, let your requests be made known unto God." (Phil. 4:6) Which then continues, "and the peace of God, which passeth all understanding, shall keep your hearts and minds through Christ Jesus." (Phil 4:7) The peace and joy the angels were so excited about is the peace and joy that comes from obeying God, thanking Him in all things, loving our enemies, praying for those that hurt us, becoming like Jesus in the inner man of the heart. Our circumstances matter nothing when we are right with God on the inside. Paul praised Him in prison.

Are we unhappy? Are there people that seem to ruin our lives? Are there circumstances in our life we just can't stand? Praise God! If we will learn to praise and thank Him for the testing, we will begin to find the secret path to inner joy and peace. When our heart's response becomes one with the Holy Spirit, and we are loving and gracious in the face of adversity and difficult situations because we have chosen to die to the flesh that would react apart from God, then not only peace and joy are ours, but the power of God becomes activated on our behalf to bless, protect, help, and lift us up. No wonder the angels were excited!

Trust In the Unseen Things of God

Heavenly Father, You are kind and understanding beyond what we deserve. We are grateful for Your guidance, faithfulness, and generosity toward us. We falter all too often in the challenges presented to us. Grant us grace and strength to better respond to the winds of life, which blow against our souls. Preserve our faith until the day of Thy soon coming. Gird us with determination to do Thy will alone. May our time, each moment of it, be spent to further Your desires here on earth. In Jesus's name we pray. Amen.

Weaning The Soul in Preparation for The Holy Spirit

Following the devastating crucifixion and burial of the Lord Jesus, the believers He left behind struggled with the events that had so rapidly transpired. They had experienced, in just a few days, the miracle working power of His presence, His trial and crucifixion, and His burial. Then, when they went to the grave with spices, He was gone! As two of them walked and communed on the road to Emmaus, He joined in their discussions. They were confused. They thought He would have redeemed Israel, which had not happened. (Luke 24:21) He was missing from His grave and was reported to be alive. (Luke 24:23) After Jesus responded and explained the scriptures to them, they recognized Him, but then He disappeared.

As they rushed to tell the apostles, Jesus Himself joined them again. Their response was, "they were terrified and affrighted, and supposed that they had seen a spirit." (Luke 24:37)

Jesus spent considerable time convincing them He was indeed the risen Lord. He showed them His hands and feet, and shared food with them. We are told "then opened He their understanding, that they might understand the scriptures." (Luke 24:45) The concept of the death and resurrection of Christ was difficult for even His closest followers. They struggled with it. In Luke 24:50-51, we read that Jesus was then taken up from them into heaven. However, this was not immediately after first reappearing to them. (At that point they were in no shape to be left alone as His messengers!) The event took place forty days later! For over a month following His resurrection, and prior to His final ascent into heaven, Jesus spent time with His disciples. In Acts 1:3 we read, "To whom also he shewed himself alive after his passion by many infallible proofs, being seen of them forty days, and speaking of the things pertaining to the kingdom of God." Verse two refers to these disciples as being the apostles. It took more than one appearance of Jesus to establish in these men what God desired. Jesus worked with them for forty days getting them prepared for what lay ahead. He also instructed them, as we read in Acts 1:4, "commanded them that they should not depart from Jerusalem, but wait for the promise of the Father, which, saith he, ye have heard of me. For John truly baptized with water, but ye shall be baptized with the Holy Ghost not many days hence." Jesus was preparing them to move into the realm of the unseen. He would be gone from visual sight, but the Holy Spirit would come to them. The Holy Spirit of God would empower them, teach them, lead them, and guide them. This was the plan all along! To reunite lost man to God directly, one on one, through the Spirit of God coming into man. As the Spirit had been in Jesus, so now He was to be in every believer.

Between His first appearance to the apostles, and being taken up to heaven, Jesus confirmed His resurrection to this group by many infallible proofs. (Acts 1:3) He would not leave it to just one brief meeting. He worked to be sure they understood the depth of what had happened. By repeated confirmation, He wanted them totally convinced of the events and their meaning. Then would they be unwavering to move in the power of the Holy Spirit who was being sent to them from the Father after Jesus's departure. We do not read of any Jewish non-believers being upset about His presence during these forty days. His appearance was to those who believed, not the world in general. (The rulers of the Jews seem to have been completely blind to these appearances.)

There was also another motive in Jesus's frequent appearances to his disciples. As He seems to have made appearances to them, and then disappeared from them for periods of time, (Luke 24:31 & John 21:1), it was as though He was weaning them from relying upon His visual flesh and bone person. He wanted their faith to be in the unseen realm of God the Father. The more he appeared repeatedly, resulting in the summation of many infallible proofs, (Acts 1:3) Jesus established their faith in preparation for the ministry of the Holy Spirit. By His frequent appearing, they gained a comfort that indeed He was nearby, always. (See John 20:19-31 and John 21:1-14)

Jesus knew the ministry of the Holy Spirit would require this weaning from His physical presence. He had to prepare them for His departure. Even the angels gently admonished them to stop gazing into Heaven, after His ascension, as He would one day return. (Acts 1: 10-11) How kind is our God in His dealing with us! Those of us who have believed without having been in His flesh and bone presence, have been brought directly into the relationship God planned. By believing in Jesus as Savior, upon the hearing of His word, we were born again into the family of God in the Spirit. However, we may still need some weaning experiences. We yet need our eyes trained to focus upon Him in the realm of the unseen, and not falter into trusting in the things seen. Is there something in our lives we look to more than to Jesus? If there is, God will work to wean us from our dependencies also. God will be as gentle with us, as with the apostles, if our heart's desire is to yield our will to Him and draw closer to Him. When all we see is vanished, and we stand before God, will our faith have been in Him alone? If all were taken from us tomorrow, are we confident in our standing with the Lord? If the answer is yes, then we are at least partially weaned from trusting in things other than Jesus.

When we trust in God in the Spirit, we move in the same way Jesus did. What He suffered from unbelief and misunderstanding; we will suffer. As His followers began preaching salvation through faith in the name of Jesus, then were the non-believers riled to persecute the disciples of Christ. The mantle had been shifted, from Jesus to His followers. They were now the messengers! They were moving in His power and receiving the attacks from the enemy of light. Jesus knew His disciples would need their faith strengthened in the things of God not seen in the natural. They had to learn to be confident in His nearness, though not visible, and they required the power of the baptism of the Holy Spirit to be victorious. So do we!

For They Know His Voice

John 10:4

Heavenly Father, in this time of so many voices seeking to direct our paths, we ask You to teach us of Your voice. We ask to always be given a hunger and thirst for the things of the Spirit and to learn to always yield to Your will. Help us pay the price of obedience to the Holy Spirit's call. May those who are confused find peace and light in Your presence. We pray against the powers of darkness that seek to hinder the work of the Holy Spirit, and we ask for a mighty outpouring of Your anointing upon the work that You would do. Help each of Your children to trust more in You and see You more clearly. In Jesus's name we pray. Amen.

In the tenth chapter of John, Jesus gives us a beautiful description of Himself as the Good Shepherd. These passages tell of His great love for His followers, in that He is the only one who will lay down His life for the sheep. They explain that when the sheep are threatened, He will not leave them alone as a hired person would do. They tell of the joys of having Him as our Shepherd, saying, "By me if any man enter in, he shall be saved and shall go in and out and find pasture." (John 10:9) He further states His purpose of coming to be our Shepherd, saying, "I am come that they might have life, and that they might have it more abundantly."(John 10:10) These scriptures compare Jesus to others by describing them as thieves and robbers come to steal, kill and to destroy. Such a comparison, coupled with Jesus's description of Himself as the Good Shepherd, makes us desire Him to be our Shepherd. Knowing His promises for us, it is natural that we should want to have Him guide us and watch safely over us as we walk through the pastures of life.

One of the keys to finding ourselves in His pasture is to know His voice. Hearing and following His voice will lead us into the safe pastures of life. The sheep Jesus describes in John 10 know his voice, and also know when the voice is *not* His. "And when he putteth forth his own sheep, he goeth before them, and the sheep follow him: for they know his voice. And a stranger will they not follow, but will flee from him: for they know not the voice of strangers." (John 10:4-5) How then can we know His voice? How can we discern the difference between the many voices competing for our attention: the voice of the flesh, the voice of other people, the voice of the evil one, the voice of religious humans, and the voice of the Holy Spirit? How often we can look back to past experiences and see much more clearly than looking forward. It is easy to look back upon our mistakes and see when we listened to the wrong voice. The heart's cry of the one seeking to follow Jesus is to move forward with the same clear vision we have when looking back. The secret is in learning to know Him and His voice; then the counterfeit will likewise be discerned.

By example in scripture, Jesus reveals Himself to us. We know that above all else He placed the highest priority on obedience to the Father. We also know that He placed the least priority on His own will: continually dying to His own wishes and choosing to always obey the Father's will. To say it in the simplest way possible, we will know His voice when we yield control of our lives to Him. We will know His voice if we read His word and spend time with Him alone in prayer and worship. The less of this we do, then the more susceptible we will be to the influences of other voices.

Decisions to follow Jesus's voice are not always easy. There is a price of surrendering all to Him that is very real, and often reaches to the depths of our hearts. Obedience to Him does not necessarily bring peace among people. On the contrary, the more Jesus obeyed the Father, the more people were moved against Him. Jesus said in Luke 12:51-53, "Suppose ye that I am come to give peace on earth? I tell you, Nay; but rather division; for from henceforth there shall be five in one house divided, three against two, and two against three." This is one example of the price of obedience.

There are many sheep in the pastures around us. Many sheep follow many different voices. We should not think it strange that at times we seem to walk alone. Jesus said, "Enter ye in at the strait gate; for wide is the gate, and broad is the way, that leadeth to destruction, and many there be which go in thereat; because strait is the gate, and narrow is the way, which leadeth unto life, and few there be that find it." (Matt. 7:13-14) It should come as no surprise that many people follow the voice of humanity more than the voice of the Spirit. This is true because not many of us are willing to pay the price to spend sufficient time alone with God in prayer, worship, and in the study of the word to be able to discern the voice of God. Therefore, it is easier to listen to the voice of someone we presume to be telling us what God wants us to hear. To try and test the voice is not something we can do without spending time alone with Jesus.

All the sheep belong to God. As the sheep make up their own minds as to which voice they will follow, we should not be influenced by the pathway another person chooses. Ours is to seek to know His voice and to obey Him regardless of the cost. In his letter to the Galatians, Paul marveled that the sheep had chosen to follow a stranger's voice. He spoke powerfully to help them focus again upon Jesus and the work of the Holy Spirit. In1 Corinthians, Paul addressed the problem of the sheep looking to the leaders rather than to Jesus, for they were saying, "I am of Paul...I am of Apollos." (I Cor. 3:4) Some will always listen to a stranger's voice, for they will never sit still long enough to learn of His voice. Jesus wants us to know His voice. He wants us to obey His voice. If we will, then we can perhaps be of assistance to others in reminding them to keep their eyes upon Jesus and none other. It is important to teach others not to trust in religious groups or the charisma of any given leader, but to trust in the living God and the Holy Spirit who will lead, guide, and teach each and every soul that will look to Him through Jesus.

The motives of the ones hearing Jesus's voice are to see just one other soul hearing the voice of the Good Shepherd. If we fail to teach others to hear His voice, then no amount of apparent religious success is of any value. God does not want His sheep at the mercy of many voices. As the sheep are fed by the anointing of the Holy Spirit, they will know the Spirit's voice. It is better to sit with a few and hear the voice of the Spirit than to sit with hundreds and hear the voice of strangers.

As the sheep are taught to try the spirits, fewer will follow wolves in sheep's clothing. In Matthew 7, Jesus explains that many religious ministers who appear to be serving God are not His servants. He says of them, "I never knew you." (Matt. 7:23) If He never knew them, then they never knew His voice, and the sheep that followed these men were never taught to hear His voice. "By their fruits ye shall know them." (Matt. 7:20) When we see lives that are not right with God, regardless of their status, we should not follow; for they are not representatives of the voice of the Good Shepherd.

Beyond The Bend in The Road

Would you follow Him, as His child, beyond the bend in the road? Beyond that place where you may still look back upon the old ways? Or would you say to Him, "No Lord, but I will serve You from here. From here where I can still look back and ponder the pleasures of the old life, and possibly return unto them for a while." Do you not know, that beyond the bend lies many a splendor, only to be captured by those who follow? Why would you forfeit the excellency of what lies ahead for that which is not lasting? Look not back, and count not the cost, for the brave and dedicated in heart shall alone enter the promises of the Kingdom.

God purposely withholds much of what He has for you until after that first bend in the road. For beyond this point is where He desires you to walk with Him. From around the bend, you will not desire to look back any longer, for your spirit will be enraptured with the joys of Heaven, as the things of the Spirit unfold before you and your communion with Him is increased. Believe Him; there is no comparison between what is behind you and that which lies before you. The fields of the Spirit are aglow with life and beauty which surpasses that which is before the bend in the road. Do not let the cross discourage you. For yes, it is true, and it is placed in front of this bend in the road and must be. For only those who would die to the old may enter fully into the new. The pleasures of the Spirit and joys that lie beyond far surpass the pain of the cross. This is true with even Jesus, your Lord, for because of the joy that was set before Him, He endured the cross (Hebrews 12:2), that you might follow to enter His joy. Truly, His joy awaits you on the other side of the cross, around the first bend in the road. Look not back on the pleasures of what you have known in the past. Lot's wife sets an example that you cannot go any farther into the newness He has for you if you stand before the cross, looking back upon that which is behind you. Flee the old with no thought of its temporary pleasure, and God shall reward you greatly. Embrace the cross, for hidden therein is the fullness of Joy.

The Love of The Truth

2 Thessalonians 2:10

Heavenly Father, we are grateful for Your care and concern
toward us. We are thankful for Your provision and blessings
in our lives. In adversity we are thankful for our faith in
You, which helps us to see beyond the difficult moments.
Though it may seem at times that adversity will never yield,
we claim Your victory. In the times when we lack a complete
understanding of 'why', let us learn to rest in the promises of
Your word and the comfort of Your presence. With grateful
hearts we praise You. In Jesus's name we pray. Amen.

Power! Signs! Wonders! As told in 2 Thessalonians 2:9-10, all of this
can be the partner of unrighteousness, deceit, and Satan. Things
that appeared great, were not. Things that appeared religious, were
not of God. Elsewhere in scripture we see power, signs, and wonders
at the hands of Jesus. Things that appeared good, were. Things
that appeared to be of the Spirit of God were of God. (I John 4:1)
This we must do to not be deceived. And further, we are shown an
important ingredient to that which is of God: "the love of the truth."
(2 Thessalonians 2:10) scripture states that those who believed the
lie did so because they had not received the love of the truth. This is
the agape of the truth, God's love.

The love of the truth is not knowledge of the word alone. It is not

24

the adherence to religious procedures or an impressive attendance record. The agape of the truth, the core of intention from God, is the fact that God loves me as a sinner. This is what one must receive to begin to know truth in the spirit and not be deceived. One must admit his sinful state. One must see God's great unconditional love as the source of sin's forgiveness and receive it. Jesus's sacrifice, shed blood and resurrection are the proof of this love. If we reject this, we reject any real understanding of God.

How wonderful to think that God requires only that we receive the love of the truth. We are not worthy; we cannot work to become worthy; He asks only that we receive His love - the love of the truth. The love of the truth is the purpose of the truth, which is that we might be saved from sin, condemnation, and eternal torment. God's purpose in the truth is that we might have fellowship with him. How wonderful and simple. He loves me as I am and asks that I believe in this love, that I might receive His great promis es.

Those who have received this love rest in the knowledge that "God loves me and I belong to Him." Come what may, we are at peace in this love of God. Remembering that the purpose of God's love is salvation and eternal life, we then should not fear. To the degree that we have fear, we are not fully resting in the love of God. 1 John 4:18 says, "There is no fear in love; but perfect love casteth out fear: because fear hath torment. He that feareth is not made perfect in love." Fear of tomorrow paralyzes us today. Fear is a robber and a thief, taking from us today's joys and blessings. Fear shrouds us from God's love and the love of those around us. Fear and its accompanying torment are from the evil one, not from God.

No one is given to know the things of tomorrow. We must learn to rest in God's love in the now of His presence and not let the enemy rob us of our joy. If we remember God's intention, which is our salvation and eternal life with Him, we should allow no place for fear. Our destiny is sealed and secure. Storms may blow across our bow, and storm clouds may gather overhead, but there is no power that can change the promises and intentions of God concerning our soul's salvation and eternal destiny with Jesus.

We must receive the love of the truth to be saved. Truth can be studied and configured in many forms, but to receive its love requires repentance and a confession of our sins. Without this we are left with a concept that is void of God. For God is love. (I John 4:8) As we abide in His love, we will know the true signs of God.

After This Manner Therefore Pray Ye

Matt. 6:9

Heavenly Father, we have so much yet to learn and understand. We thank You for Your patience and for Your constant comfort in times of distress and challenge. We are bent toward "doing" more than toward yielding. Our activity covers over our inner needs, and they remain unsatisfied until we pause to reflect upon You. Our rushing to-and-fro masks our inner weakness and pain. Teach us to sit at Your feet that we might be healed in the inner parts of our being. Grant that we might learn more of Your ways and become more like You; not becoming more active for the sake of doing, but being filled with more of Your love and grace. In Jesus's name we pray. Amen.

The passages which follow are often referred to as the Lord's Prayer. What they represent is more of an instruction in prayer as Jesus was teaching His disciples. In Luke 11, we find Jesus responding to a request from His disciples to be taught how to pray. It is worth pondering this instruction in prayer as it reveals many things beneficial to our prayer life.

"Our Father, which art in heaven." (Luke 11:2) Here Jesus leads us to know Who we are addressing in prayer and where He abides.

He is our Father. He is not an uncaring God with no compassion for our weakness and struggles. There is a comfort and encouragement in this understanding. We can approach Him and know that as a father, He cares for us in all things that concern us. He abides in heaven. He exists in the realm of the Spirit. He is not an earthly king upon a temporary worldly throne. He rules in heaven. Therefore, it takes faith to approach Him, for by faith we see and understand the things which are not seen.

"Hallowed be thy name." (Luke 11:2) Here we see the proper heart attitude in approaching God. Hallowed means to make holy, to look upon with great respect. Thus, by praying in our hearts "Hallowed be thy name" we are humbling ourselves and acknowledging His holiness, and we approach His throne in great respect.

"Thy kingdom come." (Luke 11:2) Here a proper heart attitude is expounded upon as Jesus teaches us to have a desire for God's kingdom. We can sense an urgency in this statement, a longing for the day of His kingdom. Also, a proper perspective in prayer is gained when we acknowledge the coming of a kingdom of God quite different from that upon earth today. Our hope is in that coming kingdom, not in this world. Thus, we see much in this simple statement of thy kingdom come. This passage encourages us to have a heart that longs for God's coming kingdom, and hope for that day and acknowledge it now by faith.

"Thy will be done, as in heaven so in earth." (Luke 11:2) Certainly, God enjoys the fulfilling of His will in heaven without hindrance as the angels joyfully seek to fulfill His desires. The "in earth" request includes us as individuals in the earth, but also goes beyond to a desire for God's will and reign to be accomplished on the entire earth. We can conclude that this request is for our individual hearts as well as a desire to see the coming of the kingdom of Jesus on the earth, as promised in scripture. This passage prompts us to lay open our hearts to desire His will and not our own, as well as leading us to desire the coming of His kingdom. The two go hand in hand, for the more we desire His will, the more anticipation we have in looking for the return of Jesus to the earth to establish His rule and reign. The kingdom of the world loses its appeal the more we seek the will of the Father.

"Give us day by day our daily bread." (Luke 11:3) Jesus does not teach us to pray for a week's worth of provision, nor for a year's worth or a lifetime supply. He teaches us to pray for the needs of today. This is in keeping with His command to "take therefore no thought for the morrow: for the morrow shall take thought for the things of itself. Sufficient unto the day is the evil thereof." (Matt. 6:34) As we exercise our faith today, we shall find God's provision sufficient. And so shall we find tomorrow. We cannot eat tomorrow's bread today, for today we only have need of today's bread. Our focus should be on the now of our relationship with God.

"And forgive us our sins, for we also forgive every one that is indebted to us." (Luke 11:4) Here we are told of the operation of forgiveness, the giving and the receiving of the same. If we expect to receive God's forgiveness, He then expects us to forgive others that may have sinned against us. Thus, our hearts find a proper balance and a pleasing attitude in the sight of God.

"And lead us not into temptation, but deliver us from evil." (Luke 11:4) Here we see the progression from temptation to evil. If we yield and begin to enter into temptation, the logical conclusion is evil. By seeking to stay clear of the initial temptation, we will avoid the greater pitfall which follows. By asking to be guided away from temptation, we escape the greater need of deliverance once we are entangled. By avoiding temptation, we are indeed delivered, and with fewer consequences.

"For thine is the kingdom, and the power, and the glory, forever. Amen." (Matt. 6:13) In these simple words, as prayed from a sincere heart, we see our smallness and acknowledge God's greatness. We cast upon Him all glory, taking none unto ourselves. We acknowledge His eternal kingdom, the only true and lasting kingdom. His is not one of many kingdoms, but rather THE KINGDOM. Also, His is the power, now and forever, even though He chooses to restrain its display until a future day. All in all, Jesus threads this instruction in prayer together revealing that a humble heart and the operation of faith are essential to a productive prayer life. Such simple words hold so much more than we can see at this time.

Lord, your disciples were wise to ask for your instruction in prayer. We likewise seek your help in preparing our hearts with the proper attitude for prayer. Increase our faith and help us to see the depths of insight in Your word. In Jesus's name we pray.

There Is Therefore Now No Condemnation

Romans 8:1

Heavenly Father, your word is deep with meaning and wisdom, and yet for all our learning we merely scratch the surface of understanding the riches of knowing You. We concur with Paul's words, "for now we see through a glass, darkly, but then face to face: now I know in part; but then shall I know even as also I am known." (1 Cor. 13:12) We are quick to misunderstand and misjudge. For this we seek Your help. We measure with a partial understanding and thus build incorrect conclusions about our own life and the lives of others. Free us from these faults we pray. Let us trust and have faith in You in what is built within our hearts, as we leave with You the things we do not perfectly understand. You are working within the framework of eternity, while our inclination is to reason and conclude within the framework of our small experiences. Share with us Your perspective as we bring our hearts to You. We praise You and thank You for Your love and the ever-present Holy Spirit who is our teacher. Help us to be good students with an ear to hear the things of the Spirit. In Jesus's name we pray. Amen.

Before we can come to know God, we must acknowledge that we are sinners and ask His forgiveness, believing in the cleansing power of Jesus's blood and His resurrection from the dead. To truly be sorry for our sins means that we must see ourselves as inadequate and unworthy to approach God of ourselves, and therefore we see the error of our own way. We acknowledge that we are not perfect, we are not righteous, and that we are in need of help. We must confess this to begin our relationship with God. (1 John 1:9).\ Seeing our sins and confessing them is necessary, but then we must also learn to accept our cleansing as complete even though we do not manifest perfection in our lives. The cleansing work of Jesus on the cross is final and perfect for all who believe. We must learn to place ourselves in that position with Christ, as being accepted by the Father because of His sacrifice for us. It profits us nothing to labor beneath the burden of unworthiness, which we would wrongly hold upon our shoulders, when we are freed from sin through our faith in Jesus. Psalms 103:12 reads, "as far as the east is from the west, so far hath he removed our transgressions from us." We must accept this to enjoy our freedom from sin.

Romans 8:1 says, "There is therefore now no condemnation to them which are in Christ Jesus, who walk not after the flesh, but after the Spirit." This scripture states that *now* there is no condemnation. Not later when we are perfect; not later when we go to be with the Lord; not once we get everything just right and make no further mistakes, but now, today, we are not condemned if we are in the Lord. How wonderful this is to know. We may not understand why things transpire the way they do. We may struggle daily with the flesh man of sin. We may feel very inadequate. We may be assailed with the thoughts and judgments of others. We may be seeking that place of knowing God's perfect will for our lives and often feel that somewhere we missed something. But praise God that now, today, while we travel through a wide array of experiences, there is no condemnation from Him upon our lives, if we seek to dwell in His Spirit.

Our path may be through deep and dark valleys where we wonder if the sun will ever shine again. Our hearts may be wrenched with the pains and struggles of that which life deals to us, but we are assured that whatever our experiences in life, we are not under condemnation from the Lord if we seek His face. We may suffer the condemnation of others and be misunderstood, but this is not condemnation from above.

At times it may seem that what we feel must be God's condemnation. We look at our sin and weakness, and in ignorance we hold to that which Jesus has already taken away in the power of His love. If we look to our man of flesh and sin and admit the need for cleansing but do not turn to Jesus to receive our forgiveness, then we are choosing to stand in unnecessary guilt. Unbelief clouds our view of God's promises.

It takes an effort to walk after the Spirit. It takes a willful effort of worship, prayer, and praise to scatter the clouds of darkness that would seek to cover the Christian with condemnation. Romans 8:6 says that life and peace are for those who are spiritually minded. Peace is life without condemnation and without the burden of guilt for sin. Having once received the Lord as Savior, this place of living is for those who would continue in a life of prayer and praise. It is impossible to feel condemned when one is praising God. In true worship one is lifted above the thoughts of self and sin into the glorious acceptance of the Father. It is in this position in Christ that freedom from sin is a reality and prayer can be offered, in faith believing. In worship we understand how much He has done for us. In worship we see that He will answer our prayers. In worship there is no power that can destroy us, condemn us, or keep us from that wondrous relationship with God. In worship we are empowered to face the challenges of our days with victory; without worship we are lucky to survive them. Without prayer and worship, it is very difficult to walk after the Spirit. In the words of a song, we see the benefits of worship:

To Thee to Praise Thy Name I Come (Lyrics by Lex Adams)

When my heart is... heavy laden and I can't seem to carry on.
When I can't see...the way that clearly and my hope is nearly gone.

Chorus:

To Thee... to praise...
Thy name I come! (twice) I Lift my hands
I lift my song
To Thee... Lord... To Thee
In my hour of ... utter darkness when the light of hope is gone When
the answers... just escape me and I feel so all alone.

(Chorus)

In the power...of Thy presence when my soul is praising You. Then
the darkness... has no power as Thy light comes blazing through.

I Have Yet Many Things To Say Unto You, But Ye Cannot Bear Them Now

John 16:12

Heavenly Father, You are unchanging in Your faithfulness. You are truly the rock upon which our salvation stands sure. The winds of confusion may blow to-and-fro over the sea of humankind, yet in You there is stability and safety from the storm. Focus us upon those things which are eternal that we may build, and be built up, in the Spirit. Grant us the discernment to know the things which are of You and let us shun that which comes from any other source. Keep us unto the day of Your coming. In Jesus's name we pray. Amen.

Jesus, in speaking as he did in John 16:12, displays the understanding of the spiritual condition and abilities of those to whom He was speaking. He who was teaching knew what could be handled by those being taught. There were things which the hearers could not bear. They could not lift or handle certain things yet. One could envision a young child attempting to pick up and use the sword of a soldier. While His audience may have been comprised of adults, Jesus knew their stature of spiritual maturity and did not give them what they could not handle.

Paul, a great teacher gifted by the Holy Spirit, shared similar statements. In 1Cor. 3:2 we read Paul saying, "I have fed you with milk, and not with meat: for hitherto ye were not able to bear it, neither yet now are ye able. For ye are yet carnal." With all the great and exciting teachings of Jesus, there was also a frankness which let those who would hear know where they really stood. With Paul, there was also this straightforward honesty which promoted spiritual maturity. In Hebrews 5:13 Paul says, "For everyone that useth milk is unskillful in the word of righteousness: for he is a babe. But strong meat belongeth to them that are of full age, even those who by reason of use have their senses exercised to discern both good and evil."

Spiritual maturity comes only one way, the way of the cross. Through the crossing of the will, God makes more of His likeness visible in the believer. Paul states in 1 Cor. 3:3 that some of the believers were carnal. They were babes in the Spirit. They were thinking they had attained a spiritual level which in truth they had not. They had not yet been through the inner yielding to God through the work of the Spirit. They were zealous concerning godly things, but zeal does not equate to spiritual maturity.

A look through the first book of Corinthians reveals that there were spiritual gifts operating, but not orderly and not for the proper reasons. By reading chapter 13, one gets the clear impression that love was not the motive behind the gifts, as Paul spends a great deal of time speaking on this subject. In chapter 14, he admonishes all things to be done unto edifying, decently, and in order. Earlier in the book we are told it was commonly reported there was fornication among the church. There was arguing and disputing between brethren resulting in the equivalent of lawsuits. (Chapter 6) There was ignorance concerning participation in offerings to idols (chapter

8) As we put all of this together, we get a picture of widespread spiritual immaturity and the resulting confusion. But then we also see Paul. God had a voice to help sort out all of the mess and get things on the right track. We also see God's love and patience through Paul. We can sense Paul's love for the Corinthians, as he endeavors to correct them and build them up. He often calls them brethren, displaying his oneness with them in their growth and learning.

Doing God's will in yielding to the work of the Spirit is to let go of what we want to do for Him. Starting out on the road to spiritual maturity is not to necessarily head off to a foreign mission field or give up all responsibility to serve God full time. There is an excitement to some of these ideas that may well be quite the opposite of the crossing of our will in yielding to the cross. Seeing and believing is only the beginning. Moses knew his people needed deliverance and felt he would help them. It was forty years later that all things were ready.

And what is yielding to the cross? It is most likely not a grand and spectacular sacrifice, but rather it is found in the everyday common places of life. It is the daily event used with mastery by the hand of God to touch us inwardly where He sees we need to change. It is the thing which humbles us in our own sight. It is the circumstance which guides us to give up some cherished plan or earthly treasure, while God watches to see how gracefully we yield it up to Him. It is the thing which reveals to us that we sought to better our own reputation rather than glorify Jesus. It is the thing which comes to put to death our pride-filled ambitions which seek the accolades of man. It is the pressure that stretches us inwardly to make more room for the new wine of the Spirit. It is all the little things which add up to empty our selfishness and replace it with the character of God as described in 1 Cor. 13:4-7.

There is no way to rush growth in the spirit. Believers can be unwittingly misled by teachings concerning the gifts of the Spirit premature to the realization of a maturity level that would allow them to bear the responsibility of the gifts they seek. The laying on of hands is not a casual showing of concern. Nor is it to be carelessly encouraged. It is an ordained spiritual activity carrying the power of God and requires a preparedness to stand against the evil in the spiritual realm that would assail another. The gift of knowledge is not an inquisitive guessing game of "do you have a problem with this or that", but rather a sacred and divine revelation given to accomplish a specific work. There is no doubt in it when it is from God. Some workers may attempt to imitate the concept of the gift, not realizing the difficulty they may bring upon the soul of another through their ignorance and error. When we see these things, are we not witnessing the same disorderly activity which Paul wrote to correct in Corinth? If the teaching emphasis is on the strong meat activity of maturity, there must first have been the milk of the word. There must first have been an embracing of the crucified life. There must be a discernment from the teachers as to what others can bear, or we will find children in the Spirit seeking to use the weapons of the soldier.

God Wants a Relationship!

Heavenly Father, we are in constant need of divine light by which to see and learn from the circumstances and events of life. We cheapen the glorious sacrifice of Christ on the cross by wrongly applying our own untransformed thinking and energy to the holy work of the Spirit. You sent your Son to die for us. He willingly sacrificed Himself and shed His blood to purchase our salvation, and to cause us to know You personally. Establishing the relationship between God the Father and many believing children individually, for eternity, was accomplished on the cross. Forgive us for tarnishing this great purpose with efforts born out of any source other than that relationship with the Spirit you died and bled to give us. Grant that our focus may be on knowing You, obeying You, and yielding to You. And if any activity is commenced, grant that it be born out of the Spirit and our relationship with You, not our lower untransformed nature. In Jesus's name we pray. Amen.

Not Everyone Who Saith unto Me, Lord, Lord, Shall Enter into The Kingdom of Heaven (Matt. 7:21)

These words of Jesus can be troubling, and they should be. They should cause us to think seriously about where we stand in light of our eternal salvation, and to examine closely our works (or that which we believe to be works) for the Lord. Calling upon Him as Lord is insufficient to purchase our eternal salvation. Heaven is reserved for those who do the will of the Father, who is in Heaven. The will of the Father is that we believe in Jesus as Savior, believe in His shed blood to cleanse our sins, believe in His resurrection from the dead, repent of our sins and be born again in the Spirit. Heaven's purposes are to be manifest in our lives now, as we live daily, as this proves that we belong to Him and are heaven bound. We cannot get there by our works, but our lives should bear out the works of heaven if we are doing the will of God.

Jesus acknowledges that many are confused and will remain so until heaven escapes them. They will die not having come to understand the will of the Father. They will have missed their precious chance to know God and eternal life. And these of which he spoke were not the blatant unbelievers and outwardly sinful, but rather the religious, the doers of good things. He says, "Many will say to me in that day, Lord, Lord, have we not prophesied in thy name? and in thy name have cast out devils? And in thy name done many wonderful works?" (Matt. 7:22) These words are amazing to our religious lower nature. We wrestle with them as to argue with God, reasoning, "You mean I can preach about God, do spiritual works, and be involved in many good works toward humankind, for my church, and for the world, and yet miss heaven?" Yes! This is precisely Jesus's point. The Lord's answer to this argument was simple and profound. "And then will I profess unto them, I never knew you: depart from me, ye that work iniquity." (Matt. 7:23) We must never let ourselves be confused as to God's purpose… Relationship! What is our relationship with Him? How well do we know Him personally? Are we getting to know Him better in our pilgrimage through life, or are we too busy with good activity to allow Him intimate entrance into our lives?

Jesus cuts straight to the heart of the confusion. Religious activity is nothing, relationship is everything. Any good that comes from the life of a Christian comes as a result of a personal relationship with Jesus, not from noble efforts to do good or religious things. This is the problem with too many of us today. We are motivated to religious action to somehow justify ourselves before God. We derive a sense of release from guilt and justification that we are godly by works rather than relationship. Even those who have begun to know Him and are heaven bound may yet enter the ranks of the confused by replacing yielding and obedience with religious activity. Paul spoke to the Galatians admonishing, "Are ye so foolish, having begun in the Spirit, are ye now made perfect by the flesh?" (Gal. 3:3) Once we are introduced to Jesus by the Holy Spirit, we must remain on the Spirit's course, which is focused on causing us to know God the Father better. It is a message of darkness which promotes activity outside of God Himself. God is never the one pushing us into activity. He is drawing us to come to know Him better, so that we may behold the works which He desires to accomplish. There is a great difference between religious activity and knowing God.

If we never come to know Jesus on a personal level, our soul will suffer eternal torment. If we do know Him and launch out into activity without Him or seek to substitute religious works for yielding and obedience to Him, we will suffer the loss of even the works we think we have accomplished. (1 Cor. 3:11-15.)

We by nature are not very good at sitting still. It is easier to be doing things than to deepen our relationship with God. We are easily thrown out of focus with God's priorities. To make us one with Him, to mold us into His likeness that we might know Him, these are God's priorities. What are ours? Are they to build and do great things, or to achieve a sense of accomplishment? Or are we willing to let our own energies be pressed through the cross until we have none of our own and are fit for God's purposes? There is great joy in the common places of life when we can learn to see the work of God there.

Jesus declared "I never knew you, depart from me." (Matt.

7:23) As we see that He desires for us to know Him, we can better understand His displeasure with our activities which stand in the way of our relationship with Him. May we learn to say 'depart from me' to all efforts of self which keep us from a deeper relationship with Jesus. Wrongly sourced activity may give us a sense of appeasing God or self-satisfaction that we are okay with God, but only obedience and knowing Him will bring lasting peace and joy. When our focus is correct, we can find great joy in the most unspiritual settings, for we find Him there.

Conversely, death and rejection are to be found in the greatest of religious works if He does not know them. Relationship is everything to the Father. The Son sacrificed Himself to spiritually introduce us to the Father. The price paid emphasizes the importance to God. We are wise to ponder and learn the will of the Father. Does He know us? Does He know our works; that is, are they born of our relationship with Him through the prompting of the Holy Spirit?

Ye Shall Be Baptized with the Holy Ghost

Acts 1:5

So, what does this mean, we will be baptized with the Holy Spirit? Have we been around fringe believers who have turned us away from the moving of and gifts of the Spirit? Have we been taught against the gifts of the Spirit? Has it just seemed too hard to understand and accept, so we have decided to ignore it? Or have we desired this baptism of the Spirit and have just not been able to receive it?

The scriptures foretold that the believer would be baptized with the Holy Ghost, through the words of our Lord in Acts 1:5, as well as the testimony of John the Baptist when he said, "He shall baptize you with the Holy Ghost and with fire." (Matt. 3: 11) It is essential to have a clear understanding of what the baptism of the Holy Spirit is, or we stand to miss out on an important dimension of the Christian life. One of the basic questions to answer is, "Does the baptism of the Holy Spirit come at the same time as salvation, or is it a separate experience?" If we hold that it is not a separate experience, then we have no need to further seek for the baptism of the Holy Spirit. While it is possible to receive the baptism of the Spirit simultaneously with salvation, from scripture we find that this is not the normal case as we will see.

In Acts we read what Jesus's words to the apostles, who were already believers, had fellowshipped with the risen Lord Jesus and were heaven bound. "Being assembled together with them, commanded them that they should not depart from Jerusalem, but wait for the promise of the Father, which saith he, ye have heard of me. For John truly baptized with water; but ye shall be baptized with the Holy Ghost not many days hence." (Acts 1:5) In verse eight of this same chapter, the baptism of the Holy Spirit is spoken of as "the Holy Ghost coming upon you." (Acts 1:8) The meaning is the same. In all Scriptural accounts except one, the baptism of the Holy Spirit, or the coming of the Holy Ghost upon man, is referred to as something happening to the believer after salvation.

To better understand the baptism of the Holy Spirit, we will look at the examples where it is recorded in the book of Acts. In Acts 2:1-4 we read, "And when the day of Pentecost was fully come, they were all with one accord in one place. And suddenly there came a sound from heaven as of a rushing mighty wind, and it filled all the house where they were sitting. And there appeared unto them cloven tongues like as of fire, and it sat upon each of them. And they were all filled with the Holy Ghost and began to speak with other tongues, as the Spirit gave them utterance." This initial baptism, which Jesus had promised, was accompanied by the speaking in other tongues. This manifestation was also foretold by Jesus in Mark 16: 17 when He said, "These signs shall follow them that believe ... they shall speak with new tongues." Of significance in this account of the outpouring of the Holy Ghost is the fact that God fashioned cloven tongues as of fire as a sign of what was taking place. God could have chosen any figure to accompany this outpouring, such as a dove, but He chose cloven tongues as of fire. When we couple this with other accounts of the baptism of the Holy Spirit, seeing that they too were mostly witnessed with the speaking forth in tongues, it seems evident that God is placing some measure of importance upon the speaking in other tongues. (Not that tongues is the baptism of the Holy Spirit, but rather a manifestation of the baptism of the Holy Spirit.)

Peter refers to this event as a fulfilling of the prophecy of Joel in Acts 2:17, "'And it shall come to pass in the last days,' saith God, 'I will pour out of My Spirit upon all flesh.'" In Acts 2:18 we also read, "And on my servants and on my handmaidens, I will pour out in those days of my Spirit." While scripture says they would be baptized with the Holy Ghost, Peter and Joel say it is a pouring out. The terminology is secondary to the fact that there is indeed a second spiritual experience after salvation for the believer. Peter concludes by saying to those to whom he preached, "Repent, and be baptized every one of you in the name of Jesus Christ for the remission of sins, and ye shall receive the gift of the Holy Ghost." (Acts 2:38-39) Repentance and remission of sins brings us salvation, and the gift of the Holy Ghost is additional. To say that the baptism accompanies salvation is to say that the apostles were not saved until the day of Pentecost, which violates the foundation of salvation through faith in Jesus Christ and his shed blood and resurrection.

Was this baptism experience at the day of Pentecost only for the apostles, or is it for the believer today? Peter again clarifies by stating in Acts 2:39, "For the promise is unto you, and to your children, and to all that are afar off, even as many as the Lord our God shall call." The baptism of the Holy Spirit is for all believers.

It is important to state that the baptism of the Holy Spirit is given so that the Christian might live and minister in the power of the Spirit of God. Jesus commanded the apostles to wait for it; it was not optional for them. He said they would receive power after the Holy Spirit was come upon them. As they needed this power for service, so we need the same power. The baptism is not to be sought as a spiritual experience of itself, nor for an emotional high. It is given to further the work of God through the believer. God gives the Holy Spirit to those who obey Him. (Acts 5:32) This means that our life is laid down to do His will. The heart of the believer is saying by asking for the baptism of the Holy Spirit, "Lord, I am yours completely, Thy will be done in me. I want everything you have for my life. Lord, here am I." Receiving the baptism of the Spirit is not to be tested with one's feelings, for it is an act of faith in accord with God's word. baptism experiences will range from feeling nothing to electrifying. The purpose is not to give feelings, but to give power to the Christian to live in the Spirit and minister in the power of the Spirit in whatever capacity God purposes.

The next account of the baptism of the Spirit is in Acts 8:5-17. From this passage we see clearly again that the people receiving the baptism had already believed in God through the preaching of Philip, and had already been baptized in water in the name of the Lord Jesus. We then read in Acts 8:14-17; "Now when the apostles which were at Jerusalem heard that Samaria had received the word of God, they sent unto them Peter and John: who, when they were come down, prayed for them that they might receive the Holy Ghost: (For as yet he was fallen upon none of them: only they were baptized in the name of the Lord Jesus). Then laid they their hands on them, and they received the Holy Ghost." Here the Holy Spirit didn't just fall upon the people, but rather the apostles prayed for them that they might receive Him. Through the apostles' prayers and laying on of hands, the Holy Ghost was given. There are some who say that the baptism of the Holy Spirit should not be asked for, because God will give it when He wants. However, this does not agree with the words of Jesus in Luke 11: 13, "If ye then, being evil, know how to give good gifts unto your children; how much more shall your Heavenly Father give the Holy Spirit to them that ask Him?" While this account of the baptism doesn't say they spoke with tongues, neither does it say that they did not speak with tongues. But it is worth noting that Simon offered the disciples money to have the power to baptize people with the Holy Spirit. (Acts 8:18-19) What did he observe that would cause him to say this? I believe he observed the same thing that the Jewish believers saw when Cornelius and his family were baptized with the Holy Spirit in Act 10, as we read next.

We read of another account of the baptism of the Spirit in Acts 10:44-47, "While Peter yet spake these words, the Holy Ghost fell on all them which heard the word. And they of the circumcision which believed were astonished, as many as came with Peter, because that on the Gentiles also was poured out the gift of the Holy Ghost. For they heard them speak with tongues, and magnify God. Then answered Peter, 'can any man forbid water, that these should not be baptized, which have received the Holy Ghost as well as we?' " This account shows us that salvation and the baptism of the Spirit can happen at the same time, for as the hearers believed on the word preached, God baptized them with the Holy Spirit. It is interesting to note that the way in which the Jews knew that these people had received the baptism of the Holy Ghost was that they heard them speak with tongues and magnify God. Peter later gives an account of this happening in Acts 11:15-16 saying, "And as I began to speak, the Holy Ghost fell on them as on us at the beginning. Then remembered I the word of the Lord, how that he said, John indeed baptized with water, but ye shall be baptized with the Holy Ghost." Thus, Peter affirms that the baptism of the Holy Spirit was a part of the Gospel to the Jews as well as the Gentiles. Some may take the stance that if God wants to baptize me with the Holy Spirit, He can come upon me just like them. This may be true, for God is certainly able, but the heart attitude is incorrect. One could also say that if God wants my attention, He can slay me to the ground in a bright light just like He did Paul. Such an attitude is tempting God and rebellious. Further, the word commands us to not go to the work of the Lord without first having received the power of the Holy Spirit through the baptism of the Holy Spirit. (Acts 1:4-5)

Now look in Acts 19:1-7 to the record of the baptism of the Spirit when Paul found certain believers in Ephesus. Here the Spirit didn't just fall, but rather Paul asked them if they had received the Holy Spirit since they believed. We then find again that the Holy Spirit is given through prayer and the laying on of hands. Also, we see the baptism accompanied with speaking in tongues and prophecy.

To receive the baptism of the Holy Spirit, we should first come to where we desire to do God's will and not our own. Acts 5:32 says that the Holy Spirit is given to those who obey God. Next, we should ask, even as we are encouraged in Luke 11: 13. In Mark 11:24 we are admonished to pray, believing we shall receive, "What things soever ye desire, when ye pray, believe that ye receive them, and ye shall have them." And in I John 5:14-15, we are further told that if we ask anything according to His will, "we have the petitions that we desired of him." We know from Acts 2:39 that the promise of the gift of the Holy Spirit is God's will for all who will ever be called by the Lord. And from the command of Jesus in Acts 1:4-5, we can be assured that it is God's will that we be baptized with the Holy Spirit, and that even the very act of asking for the baptism is obeying God. If we do not desire the baptism of the Holy Spirit, then we need to ask God to cause us to desire it, for from the word it is His desire for all believers. Jesus's command to wait for the promise of the Father is yet alive for the believer today in order for us to have the power of the Spirit in the Christian life. While some argue that you always receive the baptism at salvation, and while it may be hard to grasp with the natural reason how we can receive Christ's Spirit when born again and then later receive more of the same Spirit in the baptism of the Holy Spirit, the accounts of the baptism which we have just read show clearly that the baptism of the Spirit follows salvation most of the time.

Many ask, "Why is the gift of tongues and not some other gift often mentioned in conjunction with the in-filling of the Holy Spirit?" To answer this, we must briefly examine parts of 1 Corinthians 12 and 14. Paul explains in 1 Corinthians 14 that there are two different uses of the gift of tongues. One is for the prayer life of the believer which edifies him personally. We read in 1 Corinthians 14:4, "He that speaketh in an unknown tongue edifieth himself." In 1 Corinthians 14:14 we read, "For if I pray in an unknown tongue, my spirit prayeth." Paul's statement in 1 Corinthians 14:18, "I thank God I speak with tongues more than ye all," is referring to his private use of tongues. In the next verse he states, "Yet in the church I had rather speak five words with my understanding, that by my voice I might teach others also, than ten thousand words in an unknown tongue." (1Corinthians 14:19) Paul places emphasis on the private use of tongues, and in this chapter is setting in order the use of the gifts when gathered together, admonishing the brethren not to get out of hand. The public use of tongues in a meeting requires an interpretation, as explained in 1 Corinthians 14:27. While an interpretation is required with the public use of tongues, no interpretation is required for the prayer use of tongues. In the accounts of the baptism of the Holy Ghost where there was the manifestation of tongues, there is no mention of interpretation.

It makes sense that the accounts of this manifestation were the loosening of the believers' tongues to speak in the language of the Spirit. Having once received the loosening of the tongue to speak in the Spirit, all are admonished to use the language to pray. (Eph. 6:18) The public use, accompanied by interpretation, is a different manifestation of this gift. We must realize that receiving the initial loosening of the tongue to utter words in the Spirit is the primary first step. Also, there is certainly a place for singing in the Spirit as well as worship and prayer in the Spirit within public gatherings., which may not require an interpretation. (Paul's words of letting all things be done decently and in order are the guiding principle.)

A helpful common-sense comment: When learning a foreign language, we must make the sound with our voice, move our tongue and lips to try and speak the language. Which at first may sound nothing like it should. To pray in the spirit, in tongues, takes the same effort. We must make the sound, allow our mouth and tongue to fashion syllables as we keep our eyes upon the Lord. Will it sound foolish? Yes. Our minds will not understand it. Do not let that discourage you.

While I Corinthians 12:30 is often used to substantiate that not all believers are to speak with tongues, if looked at in context, it is clear that Paul is referring to the public use of tongues. He is speaking of those gifts placed in the church. Paul never asked for an interpretation in Acts 19; neither did Peter in Acts 10. scripture seems to reveal that the reason tongues is found with the baptism of the Spirit is because the prayer use of tongues is the one gift which can be used to edify the believer. (1 Cor. 14:4) Paul must have found edification in praying in tongues for he stated he did it more than they all. And Paul, who knew the difference between praying with the understanding and praying in the Spirit (1 Cor. 14:15) admonished all believers in Ephesians 6:18, "Praying always with all prayer and supplication *in the spirit.*"

There is, therefore, every reason to ask God for the baptism of the Holy Spirit, as well as for the manifestation of speaking in tongues, as it is so consistently a part of the baptism experiences accounted for in the book of Acts. Tongues is not to become an issue. Let us get past the issue, receive the baptism of the Holy Spirit and the manifestation of tongues. Tongues becomes an issue when it is fought and resisted. Once received, it is something which is used, not argued over.

But The Holy Ghost,
He Shall Teach
You All Things

John 14:26

The Lord wants you to hear Him. Yes, to hear from Him directly. And He is working to bring this to pass…that you hear God and understand Him when He speaks or shows you something. To know for certain when He shines light on something in your life. And it is through the Holy Spirit that He does this.

Jesus died to bring about a communion between God the Father and man. Man was created by God to have fellowship with Him; but with sin, came separation from God. We are told that through the blood of Jesus we are reconciled to God through faith in His Son. When a person believes in Jesus's redemptive work on the cross, he is then brought into fellowship with the Father. (1 John 1:3) This is a holy thing, this communion of a man with the Father. It is truly likened unto the Holy of Holies where only the High Priest entered once a year to make an atonement for sin. (Hebrews 9:6-8) Paul is clear in explaining that the believer is the temple of the Holy Ghost, saying in 1 Corinthians 6:19, "What? know ye not that your body is the temple of the Holy Ghost, which is in you, which ye have of

God, and ye are not your own?" The mystery of the Gospel is truly beyond the comprehension of the natural mind when we consider that God has come to dwell within us by His Spirit.

Scripture goes on to tell us of the wondrous work of the Holy Ghost within the believer. In John 14:26 Jesus said, "But the Comforter, which is the Holy Ghost, whom the Father will send in my name, he shall teach you all things, and bring all things to your remembrance, whatsoever I have said unto you." Again, in 1 John 2:27 we read, "But the anointing which ye have received of him abideth in you, and ye need not that any man teach you: but as the same anointing teacheth you of all things and is truth, and is no lie, and even as it hath taught you, ye shall abide in Him." The Bible is clear that our teacher is the Holy Spirit of God, and truly He is the only one who can open our understanding to receive truth from the Father. This provision for the believer to receive truth from God the Father, through the Spirit, was made a reality when Jesus died and shed His blood to establish the communion between man and the Father. The price paid to establish this communications link is beyond measurement in worldly wealth; for how can we place a value upon the life of Jesus, God's Son, given in love to purchase eternal life for as many as would believe?

From the viewpoint of the Father, a great effort has gone into making communion possible between Himself and humankind. It is no light matter that we become the temple of the living Spirit of God when we are born again. We must understand this point clearly to fully comprehend the ministry of the Holy Spirit through humankind today.

The same Bible which tells us that we need have no human teach us, also says that God has raised up some humans to help others grow in the Lord. We read in Ephesians 4:11-12, "And he gave some, apostles; and some, prophets; and some, evangelists; and some, pastors and teachers; for the perfecting of the saints, for the work of the ministry, for the edifying of the body of Christ." Because God has chosen to speak to others through humans as described above in Ephesians, there is a great need to understand how God works through a human so that the believer is not deceived. The believer must clearly see the intentions of God to know those that speak of God's Spirit and those that do not.

One thing must be remembered: Jesus died to establish the communications between the believer and God the Father. Therefore, if someone is speaking in the Spirit of God, he will be helping to further establish the communications which Jesus died to create. At the same time, one is being used of God to fortify and expand the communications link between another and God, he/she will also realize that the communications link is truly the Holy of Holies. No man, woman, religion, organization, pastor, or priest has a right to stand between another soul and God the Father in the communications channel. To cause another to look to a person or religion in the outer is to say, "Don't trust in the communications channel which Jesus has given you; trust in something else also." To place any person or anything in the middle of the communications channel is to place something else in the seat of Christ and is sin. Only those who are sent of God are allowed of God, under the anointing of the Holy Spirit, to minister to others to build up the communications linkage which Jesus died to create. Those who are not moving under the anointing of God's Spirit will only be able to cause others to trust in outer forms of religion or personalities other than the Lord Jesus Christ.

The ministers which are described in Ephesians 4 are called by God to build up others in their faith in Jesus, not in themselves or their religious affiliations. Deception is subtle; but we must realize that if our faith is standing in strong personalities, or religious organizations, and not in Jesus Himself, then the communications between God and a person are being hindered by interference. Ministers of God should stay clear of the Holy of Holies within the heart of another, realizing that Jesus is Lord and needs no help in being Lord, but rather others need help in putting their eyes upon Him and releasing their faith in Him.

Today, the need is to help others experience the fellowship with the Father which comes through faith in Jesus. The danger is as Jesus said in Matthew 24:4-5, "Take heed that no man deceive you. For many shall come in my name, saying I am Christ: and shall deceive many." We are told that the deceivers would come in His name, not in the name of another. This is the danger. As one understands God's intention in directly desiring communion with each believer and having this communion expanded and built up by the ministry of the Holy Ghost through others, deception is less likely. If any person or religion is causing others to trust in them, no matter how good it sounds, such a one is really saying as Jesus warned, I am Christ. While we would probably not believe someone coming up to us and saying, I am Christ, yet how subtly Satan disguises himself and tries to block the communications channel between the believer and God any way he can. Satan will use religion and good people to cause others to put their faith in anything except Jesus Himself; and in so doing, God's people are being given crutches to go to the battle in place of swords and armor.

Satan realizes that if he can block direct communication with God, and stop faith from being strengthened in the power of the Holy Ghost to teach, lead, and strengthen; then he can be successful in cutting off the source of power from the Church today. As the believer is taught to trust in God through the Holy Spirit, the believer is being hooked up to the source of power-God Himself. The more the believer trusts in Jesus, the greater threat he is to the powers of darkness. The message from the pulpit today should be, "Get your eyes on Jesus and trust Him. Don't trust in any man or religion or outer religious form. Trust in the Holy Ghost in you and in the word of God." It is the anointing of the Holy Spirit which gives men power to minister, and only as communications are directly established between the believer and God, can the anointing of God's Spirit be given.

God is not pleased with those who stand in the way and prevent others from entering into full communications with God the Father through the power of the Holy Ghost. A person is not to become the interpreter of truth for others, but to cause others to trust in and know the Holy Ghost as the interpreter of truth. Much of religion today has caused people to trust in religious systems and people in religious positions, creating congregations with no power, and no live and fruitful relationship with God. By neglecting to challenge others to believe God for the moving of His Spirit in them, they have become as those spoken of by Jesus in Luke 11:52, "Woe unto you, lawyers: for ye have taken away the key of knowledge; ye entered not in yourselves, and them that were entering in ye hindered." The responsibility of any minister of God is to help others enter the fullest relationship with Jesus possible, not preventing it in any way by standing between another and the moving of the Spirit in them. When religion says, "Trust in me," it is really taking away the key of knowledge and cutting off the believer from Jesus, while appearing to come in His name.

The Bible's message for the believer today is, "You can trust in the Holy Spirit in you." Jesus didn't die to establish a poor quality of communications between God the Father and a believer. He has given the believer the Holy Spirit of God as the teacher and revealer of truth, and there could never be a better teacher. The challenge is to help others trust in God and the Holy Spirit in them so that they might know the power of the Lord to overcome and be strong, and minister in the power of the Lord's Spirit. We do well to remember the words of our Lord, "And I, if I be lifted up ... will draw all men unto me." (John 12:32) This is the ministry of the Holy Spirit; to cause others to be drawn unto Jesus.

The Inner Working
of the Holy Spirit

Do you ask yourself at times, "Why do I do things I know are wrong? Why do I react poorly to others when I know I shouldn't? Why do I lose my temper when I am supposed to be a new creature in Christ?" To help us understand what is going on in us, God has some of the answers. Being born again and accepting Jesus as our Savior is just the beginning of His work in us. We are certainly not complete in our transformation as far as living it out in the here and now, we are a work in process.

There are three areas which we will discuss concerning the inner work of the Holy Spirit in the heart of the believer. First, we will learn that there are two of each of us, the natural person and the inner or spiritual person. Secondly, we will look at the way God views us as He is maturing the spiritual person and dealing with sin in the Christian. Last, we will look at the simple process which God has established as the way in which to strengthen the inner spiritual person.

The scripture is clear that there is the natural person and the inner or spiritual person. (See 1 Cor. 2:14, Rom. 7:22) It is important to see what God's word says about what takes place in the Christian after salvation, so we can understand the work of the Holy Spirit and the proper way to view the old nature person of flesh. In Romans 7:14-24, Paul explains that there is a struggle going on for the control of his life. His flesh is warring against his inner person to bring him into bondage to the lower nature, while his inner spiritual person longs after the Lord and the way of the Spirit. In verse 17, Paul makes an important point; when he falls and sins, it is not his spiritual born again person that sins, but rather his old flesh person of sin. In 1 John 5:18 we read, "We know that whosoever is born of God sinneth not." And in 1 John 3:8 we read, "He that committeth sin is of the devil." Where then do we stand with God if we sin? Do we lose our salvation? Are we no longer born of God? For, "He who is born of God sinneth not." (1 John 5:18) The answer is NO! The key to understanding what Paul and John are saying is in I John 3:6 where we read, "Whosoever abideth in Him sinneth not." If then we abide in the Spirit with our spiritual person in control of the body by the power of the indwelling Christ, indeed we are kept from sin, for in Him is no sin. But if we abide in the lower nature flesh person, then we abide in sin and will manifest the works of the flesh and the devil. This is the struggle of which Paul speaks in chapter 7 of Romans. Our first step toward allowing the Spirit of God to control our lives is to acknowledge as Paul did that "in me, (that is, in my flesh) dwelleth no good thing'" (Romans 7:18)

A common misunderstanding is to think that because we are a new creature in Christ and all things are new, everything we do once we are a Christian is of God's Spirit. Such a stance hinders the work of God in revealing the difference between the works of the flesh and the moving of the Spirit in the Christian. Our spiritual person is indeed a new creature, but the process by which the spiritual person grows and rules over the person of flesh cannot fully start until the Christian acknowledges that he indeed has a sinful fallen nature of flesh and needs God's power working within to overcome.

Now that we know the inner struggle is going on, we need to understand how God views us as we grow in spiritual strength and learn to overcome the ways of the flesh. Romans 8:1 says, "There is therefore now no condemnation to them which are in Christ Jesus, who walk not after the flesh, but after the Spirit." If our hearts' desire is to walk after the Spirit, then as God deals with areas of our lives and reveals sin, we are viewed by God through the righteousness of His Son. The blood of Jesus is ever cleansing us as we ask forgiveness and confess our sins. Therefore, regardless of the magnitude of our inner struggle with the flesh of sin, we can stand up and claim God's forgiveness and not accept the condemnation of the devil. There is nothing the devil likes more than to condemn the Christian because of his failures and weakness in order to render him useless to God. Our usefulness in the sight of God is by faith, not by our own goodness or works.

The fact that God forgives should never give place to a casual attitude about sin and overcoming the flesh nature. In Romans 6: 11-16, Paul clearly admonishes us on this point, saying, "Likewise reckon ye also yourselves dead indeed unto sin, but alive unto God through Jesus Christ our Lord. Let not sin therefore reign in your mortal body, that ye should obey it in the lusts thereof. Neither yield ye your members as instruments of unrighteousness unto sin; but yield yourselves unto God, as those that are alive from the dead, and your members as instruments of righteousness unto God. For sin shall not have dominion over you; for ye are not under the law, but under grace. What then? Shall we sin, because we are not under the law, but under grace? God forbid. Know ye not that to whom ye yield yourselves servants to obey, his servants ye are to whom ye obey; whether of sin unto death, or of obedience unto righteousness?" Whether sin reigns in our bodies is a moment-to-moment decision for the Christian. What we were in the Lord a year ago, a month ago, or a week ago, does not mean today we will be in the Spirit. The only thing that is required to be in the flesh is to *not be in the Spirit*. There is no middle ground. We must exercise diligence daily to assure that our walk in the Spirit is constant, as discussed later in this chapter.

Paul states that the old person is dead, and we are not carnal but spiritual. (Romans 8:9) This is a true statement of fact; however, one cannot ignore the process of death by which the appetites and ways of the flesh are brought into subjection to the Spirit of God.

For, while we are new in Christ, we will ever have the inner struggle spoken of by Paul in Romans 7 until we leave this body of flesh. Our flesh is dead. The problem is that it doesn't know it and is in no hurry to get to the grave by yielding control of the vessel to the Spirit of God. Paul points to the death process in Romans 8:13 saying, "For if ye live after the flesh, ye shall die; but if ye through the Spirit do mortify (kill) the deeds of the body, ye shall live." Therefore, we find the work of God's Spirit in the Christian is to build up the inner person to dominate over the flesh person, putting him to moment by-moment death as we live unto the Lord, not allowing the flesh person to live. This is why Paul says, "I die daily." The death to the flesh and growth of the spiritual man is a continuing daily process.

In Romans 7:25, Paul states that his overcoming power and deliverance from the flesh is through Jesus Christ. How then do we personally realize this same deliverance and overcoming power of which Paul speaks? First, we must realize that when one is born again, he is born again as a babe in the Spirit. This spiritual newborn must be fed and nourished to grow. Feeding our inner person in times of fellowship is not enough. There must be a daily partaking of the Lord in prayer, worship, and reading of the word of God in order for our spiritual nature to mature. If we fed our flesh only two or three times a week, we would grow very weak. It is very similar in the Spirit concerning our inner person. Romans 8:4 says that the righteousness of God is fulfilled in our lives as we mind the things of the Spirit and not the things of the flesh. What we think on is very important, for if we will fill our minds with thoughts of the world and the flesh, then we will live to follow those things of which we partake constantly. We are to think on the things which are of God, and then will the cry of the flesh be silenced as we are occupied with the things of the Spirit, giving no place for the things of the flesh. (Romans 13:14) If we spend our time thinking of worldly treasure or pleasure, then we are feeding the flesh with fuel for his lower nature desires.

In Galatians 5:25 we read, "If we live in the Spirit, let us also walk in the Spirit." The word *walk* in the Greek means marching in military rank, keeping step. This implies the sense of discipline: and discipline is what is necessary to keep diligently praying, reading, and worshipping daily in order to allow God to make our inner man strong.

We cannot overcome of ourselves by our own efforts to be good or to be spiritual. This can only be done through the inner working of God's Spirit as we spend time with Him. Our efforts should not be to transform ourselves into the image of Christ, but rather to spend time with God so that He may transform us as we yield to Him. A closing thought: Don't try and focus on overcoming your weakness and sin, but rather focus on God and His word. God, thru the Spirit, will cause you to overcome.

His Sleeping Church

You, the Church, His Bride, must awake while there is yet time, for He needs you as a vessel of His love in these last hours. We have been given every blessing conceivable, yet we make only ourselves at ease and use His blessings that He gives mostly for ourselves alone. Our thoughts and goals are our own, and every person looks out for his own good. The dying world, those who don't know the Lord, look for hope and peace when there is none to be found. We have made ourselves comfortable in our religion while the hungry, the sick, the troubled are left alone, because few will follow Him and give up their own comfort to be His vessel....and His Church sleeps.

Oh, Bride of Christ, how it grieves His heart to see you encumbered with the cares of this life when He said in His word, "Take no thought for your life, what ye shall eat, or what he shall drink, nor yet for your body, what he shall put on." (Matt 6:25) We seek Him with half a heart and put Him second in our lives and then ask why His Spirit doesn't bless our endeavors. Child of God, He wants your life so fully meshed in His that truly His mind would be in you to speak, to minister, and to pray.

Awake from your sleep, for He has a mighty work to do in these last days. Give your life to Him completely. Leave behind those things that tie you down to the things of this world. Free yourself from all things that are not of Him and not of faith, for He is your provider. You need not rely on yourself, or others if He is to be your first love and the One who meets your every need. That which is not of faith is not of His Spirit.

As you lay down all the worldly goals and plans of your own desire, He will fill you. You are to be to Him as an empty vessel, empty of all selfish desires, that His Spirit may empower you and use you as He would choose. Your first love should be Him, not what He might bless you with or do for you. Your first desire should be yielding to His will daily that He might transform you into His image. Then, when you speak a word, pray a prayer, or minister, people will know that God has been in their midst, because He is so real in you.

Put Him first, and through your life He will teach you and lead you. You will know His love and healing in your life first-hand. Then when you minister, it will be from a full cup, from a life that has seen that the Lord is good and of plenteous mercy. He wants to become daily, moment by moment, reality in your life, closer than a brother, but this can be only as you deny yourself and give your desires to Him. Awake and repent, and then shall you truly live and He will restore His Church.

The Carnal Mind Is Enmity Against God

(Romans 8:7)

How do we correctly interpret scripture, especially those parts that are difficult to understand? How do we process and learn to accept the living power of the word, accepting it in spirit and in truth? How do we learn to discern the teachings that are of His Spirit from those that are tainted or false? Accepting our own natural limitations and an inclination to reason things in our own heads apart from the Spirit of God is a beginning, and by realizing that the evil one is always there to sow false ideas into our minds.

In the Christian walk it is very important that we not be ignorant of the ways in which the evil one tries to deceive the Christian and destroy the power of the truth. We have an adversary in the spirit which is at work to blind the Christian to the fullness of his calling in Christ and to keep the power of the Spirit of God out of Christianity today. The scripture states, "Put on the whole armor of God, that ye may be able to stand against the wiles of the devil." (Eph. 6: 11) The devil's wiles are his tricks, and he is always lying-in wait to deceive. We will look at some of the ways the evil one seeks to deceive and distort God's purpose in the Christian.

If Satan cannot keep us from believing in the Lord, he will try to muddy our understanding of the word to make our vision of the

Christian life less than what God intends. How does the evil one do this? First, we must realize that the devil uses truth to deceive. Truth which is born of the wrong spirit. We know this, for in Matt. 4:5-6 we read, "Then the devil taketh Him up into the Holy City, and setteth him on a pinnacle of the temple, and saith unto him, if thou be the Son of God, cast thyself down: for it is written, He shall give His angels charge concerning thee: and in their hands they shall bear thee up, lest at any time thou dash thy foot against a stone." Satan quoted from Psalm 91:11-12. Secondly, we must be aware that the deceitfulness of Satan does not come looking like darkness; he comes looking like light and truth. We are told this in 2 Cor. 11: 14-15: "And no marvel: for Satan himself is transformed into an angel of light. Therefore, it is no great thing if his ministers also be transformed as the ministers of righteousness."

This point brings us into the main theme of this message: Satan uses a Christian's natural reasoning mind to bring wrong interpretation to the word of God. We are told that in our flesh dwelleth no good thing (Romans 7:18) and this includes the mind of the flesh. Romans 8:7 reaffirms this by stating, "Because the carnal mind is enmity against God: for it is not subject to the law of God, neither indeed can be." We must realize that our carnal mind opposes God and cannot understand the things of God. The Christian needs to accept and say, "My carnal mind opposes God." (Later we will speak about the renewing of the mind.) Paul warns against the natural carnal mind trying to grasp the things of the Spirit of God in 1 Cor. 2:13-14: "Which things also we speak, not in the words which man's wisdom teacheth, but which the Holy Ghost teacheth: comparing spiritual things with spiritual. But the *Natural man receiveth not the things of the Spirit of God,* for they are foolishness unto him: neither can he know them, because they are spiritually discerned." The word is His, and by His Spirit He will reveal truth to us, not by our own powers of reason. As Christians, we must realize that the word of God can be handled correctly as well as incorrectly. The word can be received by faith or interpreted by the carnal intellect. The Bible speaks of some who took the word and twisted it because they couldn't understand it in 2 Peter 3:16: "As also in all his epistles, speaking in them of these things; in which are some things hard to be understood, which they that are unlearned and unstable wrest, as they do also the other scriptures, unto their own destruction." These were unlearned or ignorant about the danger of carnal interpretation of the word of God.

When the fallen, natural mind of a person (carnal mind) interprets scripture, we must realize that it is of Satan himself. Therefore, if the natural mind opposes God as we have read, then we know that such interpretation is on the side of the enemy, Satan. In Matt. 12:30 we read, "He that is not with me is against me." When Jesus was speaking to the Pharisees who were religious, correct in tradition and knowledgeable in the law, yet interpreting through their own understanding and not the Spirit, He told them, "Ye are of your father, the devil." (John 8:44) Satan uses the carnal mind of man, which is of itself in opposition to God, to obscure the true vision of truth and explain away the power of God.

The Christian must ask himself, "What spirit is bringing me what I read and what I hear? Is it my own spirit through my carnal mind, or God's Holy Spirit from the heart and transformed mind of me the believer?" Therefore, the Bible warns, "Beloved, believe not every spirit, but try the spirits whether they are of God: because many false prophets are gone out into the world." (1 John 4:1) A person may have part of his doctrine from the Spirit and part from the carnal reasoning. We therefore must learn to rely upon the Holy Spirit witnessing in our hearts to the Truth of God. This is why John points us to the Lord and admonishes us to trust in His indwelling Spirit, saying, "But the anointing which ye have received of Him abideth in you, and ye need not that any man teach you: but as the same anointing teacheth you of all things, and is truth, and is no lie, and even as it hath taught you, ye shall abide in Him." (1 John 2:27) When truth is mixed with part from the Lord's Spirit and part from human, it will lose one of several things: its power, its holiness, its purity, its simplicity. It can become mixed with the ways of the world or the deadness of religion without God's anointing. Truth spoken in the Spirit reveals and manifests the same Jesus we read of in the Bible, not one bit less of the Son of God than the word reveals.

God has a work to do through His people while we are on the earth. If we are not careful, we will hold doc trines which are born of unbelief and carnal reason. If it is written in the Bible, we must believe it as it is written, not as interpreted by a person. We must understand that our natural minds lean toward unbelief; for they cannot understand the things of the Spirit, as we have read above. If we do not realize this, we can fall short of the full vision of the Christian life and God's purpose for our lives. We must realize that unbelief forces the carnal interpretation of God's word. The natural mind cannot understand the ministry of the Holy Spirit through the gifts of the Spirit, the laying on of hands, the speaking in tongues, or the casting out of devils. Therefore, because of unbelief and reliance upon the natural understanding, the carnal mind interprets such scriptures as not for the believer today, but only for the apostles. Such interpretation is of the devil to keep the power of the Spirit out of Christianity today.

Jesus said, "These signs shall follow them that believe, in My name shall they cast out devils; they shall speak with new tongues, they shall lay hands on the sick and they shall recover." (Mark 16: 17 & 18) And in John 14:12 we read, "Verily, verily, I say unto you, He that believeth on me, the works that I do shall he do also; and greater works than these shall he do because I go unto my Father." Such scriptures need no interpretation; they speak clearly. What they do require is faith. Faith which says, "Lord, I believe your word because *it is written*. Even though my own mind cannot understand such great and wonderful things, I believe it."

There can be no question that God desires to manifest Himself through the Church today (those who believe on the Lord Jesus Christ as Savior). God does not want people praising the Christian as a theological genius or scholar because of wise carnal interpretations of scripture. God wants to manifest Himself through His people so that others will see God, not mere brilliant people. Writing to the Corinthians, Paul says the same thing (1 Cor 14:25), "And thus are the secrets of his heart made manifest: and so, falling down on his face he will worship God, and report that God is in you of a truth." The report is that *God is in you*. This takes the power of the Holy Spirit active in the believer, not mental knowledge of the word alone.

God intends His Church to be a revealing of His power, His love, and His glory today. We must understand that unbelief quenches the moving of the Spirit. One may say, "I am a Christian and I believe." That may be true in certain areas, but we must ask ourselves, "Do I believe all of the word as it is written? Do I believe in the power of the indwelling Christ *IN ME*?" In Matt. 13:58 we read where Jesus could not do many mighty works in their midst because of their unbelief. In Mark 5 we read where Jesus put away the unbelievers from Him prior to raising a young girl from the dead. What does this tell us? We must put away unbelief from our hearts and take God at His word, trusting Him for the understanding and the power of His Spirit to bear witness with His own Holy word. We must remember that it is His word, not a person's, and a person has no right to interpret the word outside of the light of the Holy Spirit.

Scripture tells us that we are to be transformed by the renewing of our minds. (Rom. 12:2) This renewing takes place by the working of the Holy Ghost within the believer. (Tit. 3:5) The Christian today needs the baptism of the Holy Spirit to accomplish this renewing. The apostles were instructed to wait for the baptism of the Holy Spirit because they needed the power of the Spirit first, then they would be witnesses for Jesus. As surely as the apostles needed the baptism, so do we today. Carnal interpretation of scripture would keep the power of the Holy Ghost and the baptism of the Spirit either in the days of the apostles only, or reduce it to an insignificant experience. Such is not God's intent. (Acts 2:38-39) There is no reason why the Christian today should not receive the prayer language of speaking in tongues just as the early Christian. God's word states that praying in tongues is an edification for the Christian; and in these days of darkness, the believer needs every source of edification he can get. (1Cor. 14:4)

We need to humble ourselves before God, receive His word as written, and release our faith in the power of the indwelling Christ. We must not be full of unbelief because of our own weakness and shortcomings, but full of faith that God by His Spirit dwells within, and He is able to do as is written in His word, through me. We are not our own, but are God's. We are purchased with a very precious price, the blood of Jesus. We have no right to limit the moving of God through us because of hardness of heart, unbelief, and reliance on our own understanding. God desires to manifest Himself through the heart of the believer. Let us believe Him.

We must view the truth, God's word, through faith and not our carnal reasoning. While a buildup of carnal knowledge of the word can build a religious appearance, it can also build self-pride in the knowledge received. Unbelief can force the carnal interpretation of those portions of scripture which are hard to understand. As we humbly receive God's word in faith, confessing that of ourselves we can do nothing, we place ourselves in the position where God can manifest Himself through the power of His Spirit within. To receive the word by faith, the carnal aspects of our mind must be put to death, not being allowed to interpret and distort God's word. The upper portion leads to the misuse of truth, while the lower shows God's intended use of truth to manifest Himself.

Faith In the Indwelling Christ

Do you sometimes feel unworthy to serve God? Do you see your weaknesses and problems as being too big and preventing you from being useful to the Lord? Do you wish you felt better about yourself as a believer so that you could serve God? Perhaps this look at Paul will encourage your heart and be of help.

The Bible admonishes the believer to have faith in God, for we read in Heb. 11:6, "without faith it is impossible to please Him." We are told in 1 Cor. 3:16, "Know ye not that ye are the temple of God, and that the Spirit of God dwelleth in you?" The area where many Christians are weak in faith is to believe God dwells within them. It is necessary that the believer be aware of God's purpose for indwelling the believer, and for the believer to have faith in the indwelling Christ. The Christian is no longer his own, but has been purchased by God to fulfill God's purpose in and through him during his life on this earth. Therefore, God seeks to open our eyes to His indwelling purpose.

Paul said in Phil. 4:13, "I can do all things through Christ which strengtheneth me." Paul was not looking upon his own flesh and weakness, nor upon his own abilities. Paul was looking to the indwelling Spirit of God through which Paul believed he could do all things, for with God all things are possible. Paul also states in Gal 2:20, "I am crucified with Christ; nevertheless, I live; yet not I but

Christ liveth in me; and the life which I now live in the flesh I live by the faith of the Son of God." Paul is saying, there is someone who has come into my being who is now living and expressing through me, and that someone is Christ, through the power of the indwelling Spirit of God. To this end is the believer called, that Christ might have free course to live in our hearts and manifest Himself through His people who have been purchased with His own blood. Because we know our own faults and sins so well, it is indeed a struggle to look beyond ourselves and release our faith in the power of the indwelling Spirit of God. However, as we continue, there can be no doubt that we are called to do just that; for without faith in the indwelling Christ, it is utterly impossible to please God to the degree that God desires. Without faith in the indwelling Christ, there can be little manifestation of God's own Person through the believer.

As we look at the life which Paul lived, which was by faith in the indwelling Son of God, we will see that God is yet desirous of manifesting His mighty hand through those who will believe. God has always manifested His power as He was leading His people. This holds true in the Old Testament as well as the New, including today, if we will believe. Paul says in 2 Cor. 5:16, "Though we have known Christ after the flesh, yet now henceforth know we him no more." We now know Him through the indwelling Holy Spirit. We are not to stand gazing up to heaven as did the disciples when Jesus ascended to the Father. (Acts 1:11) If we have faith in God in heaven only, then the responsibility of God doing His work rests with God in heaven. As we realize that God indwells the believer for the purpose of using the believer to accomplish His work, then the responsibility for believing God and for not quenching or grieving the indwelling Holy Spirit of God rests upon the believer. The believer is not responsible to do the work of God of himself but rather is truly responsible for yielding to the Spirit of God so that God might have His will and way in the believer.

Now, to the life of Paul. Paul lived the life foretold by Jesus as he learned to have faith in the Spirit within him. If anyone has reason for not believing God can use them, Paul had more. It was Paul who put Christians in prison and delivered them to death for their faith. Had Paul kept his eyes upon himself, he could have daily justified not serving God. Such unbelief would have greatly hindered God from accomplishing His purpose through Paul. In John 14:12, Jesus foretells of the manifestation of God through the believer, saying, "Verily, verily, I say unto you, he that believeth on me, the works that I do shall he do also; and greater works than these shall he do, because I go unto my father." How is this to be accomplished? It is through faith in the indwelling Christ. This is not a form of self-realization, but rather death to self and faith in the life of God which dwells in us by faith through the power of the Holy Spirit.

The Christian must realize that it is possible to be a born-again believer in the Lord Jesus and be heaven bound, and yet be hindered by unbelief. A heart of unbelief is evil (Heb. 3:12). If we do not believe God for the fullness of His manifestation through us, then we are holding on to some degree of unbelief. As Paul was preaching in Acts 14:10, he spoke forth to a lame man, "Stand upright on thy feet. And he leaped and walked." Paul didn't heal this man; he was healed by the Spirit of God. Paul believed in the power of Christ in him and as he moved in faith as directed by God, God manifested Himself. We see God manifesting Himself throughout the book of Acts. In Acts 14 we read of signs and wonders being done by the hands of the believers. Hands of flesh cannot do signs and wonders. What this tells us is that God had indeed indwelled the believers and was manifesting Himself because they had faith (faith in the indwelling Christ). Again, in Acts 19:6, we read of the baptism of the Holy Ghost being given by God to certain believers through the laying on of Paul's hands. These were human hands operating in faith and the human voice speaking in faith. Simply, it was God indwelling His people and manifesting Himself.

It is important to always recognize that the vessel of flesh (the believer) is not to be lifted up. The vessel of itself is nothing. We are not to have faith in ourselves, but in God. Jesus said in John 5:30,

"I can of mine own self do nothing." And in John 5:19 we read, "Verily, verily, I say unto you the Son can do nothing of himself, but what he seeth the Father do." This is the proper heart attitude. The believer must learn to say, "I believe God can do all things through me, but I also know that of myself I can do nothing. It is not me, but Christ that dwelleth in me." The glory belongs to God, not the vessel being used.

A life such as Paul's, lived by faith in the indwelling Christ, produces the authority of the Holy Spirit, not the authority of an individual. It was said of Jesus, "And it came to pass, when Jesus had ended these sayings, the people were astonished at his doctrine; for he taught them as one having authority and not as the Scribes." (Matt. 7:28- 29) This same authority was manifested in Paul, for we read in I Cor. 2:4, "And my speech and my preaching was not with enticing words of man's wisdom, but in demonstration of the Spirit and of power; that your faith should not stand in the wisdom of men, but in the power of God." It is possible to be ordained and schooled of men in religion and yet lack the authority of the Holy Spirit, because of a knowledge of God's word apart from faith in the indwelling Christ. There must be both knowledge and faith in God to produce the manifestation of God as was shown in Paul. Paul was bold to say, the kingdom of God is not in word, but in power. The purpose of God's word is not to gain only an educated mind, but a transformed life which manifests God, the Person of the living God. We are not saying that the study of God's word is not needful, for it is essential.

How can one receive an increased faith in the indwelling Christ? We are told in Jude 20, "building up yourselves on your most holy faith, praying in the Holy Ghost." The Bible states that there are two types of prayer: prayer with the understanding and prayer in the Spirit (1 Cor. 14:15). Because Jude does not say pray in the understanding, but rather in the Holy Spirit, he is speaking of prayer in the language given by the Holy Ghost as described by Paul in 1 Cor. 14. Paul thanked God that he spoke with tongues more than all others, and it is this man Paul that we look to as an example of God manifesting Himself by the power of the Spirit. We are also told in 1 Cor. 14 that prayer in the spirit, or tongues, is an edification for the believer. From this we can gather that praying in tongues indeed helps to increase our faith in the indwelling Christ. (We will look more at prayer in the Spirit in the next chapter.)

To live a life pleasing unto God requires knowledge of God's word, faith in God's word, and faith in the power of the indwelling and living God.

Prayer and Worship
for The Christian

The Christian can never live the life God desires without the proper personal prayer life. If God were a book, then to know Him would require study only. However, because God is a Person, to know Him requires study of His word as well as time spent with Him in prayer and worship. In this chapter we will be discussing prayer, as written in the scriptures, as well as a look at devotional praise and worship.

We have mentioned in the previous chapter that we are admonished in Jude 20 to "build up yourselves on your most holy faith, praying in the Holy Ghost." We know from scripture that the prayer given by the Holy Ghost is prayer in tongues. (See Acts 2:4 and 1 Cor. 14:14. While much has been spoken against speaking in tongues, we must rely upon the word of God more than the opinions of humans. God seeks to help the believer feel comfortable with the manifestations of the Spirit; and this takes time because we do not always understand the ways of God. It is similar to when one has a new job. For the first several weeks one feels uneasy because he is not familiar with what to do; but in time, as he learns what is expected, he becomes more comfortable with the new setting. Likewise, we need to be exposed to the things of the Spirit until we feel comfortable with them.

Much of religion today has taken man so far from the activity of the Holy Spirit as revealed in scripture (Acts & Corinthians) that many have great difficulty in accepting the moving of the Holy Ghost, even though the word of God is clear on the subject. May the Lord cause us to feel at one with Him, according to His word and the power of His Spirit, as we look at prayer in the Spirit.

The gift of tongues has two Biblical manifestations. One is for the personal prayer life of the believer as spoken of by Paul in 1 Cor. 14: 14, "If I pray in an unknown tongue, my spirit prayeth." Paul also says that the prayer use of tongues is an edification for the believer, as stated in 1 Cor. 14:4, "He that speaketh in an unknown tongue edifieth himself." The other use of the gift of tongues is the speaking forth in tongues in a gathering which is also to be accompanied with an interpretation. This public use or manifestation of God's Spirit is described in 1 Cor. 14:27: "If any man speak in an unknown tongue, let it be by two, or at the most by three, and that by course; and let one interpret." This manifestation is for the edification of the group being gathered together. No mention is made of interpretation being required for the prayer use of tongues. It is to be understood that the speaking forth in tongues with interpretation, or prophecy, is the manifestation of the moving of the Holy Spirit for the purpose of ministering to the body of believers, while the prayer uses of tongues edifies the individual.

When Paul says in 1 Cor. 14: 18, "I thank my God, I speak with tongues more than ye all," he is referring to his private prayer use of tongues; for in the next breath he says, "Yet in the church, I had rather speak five words with my understanding, that by my voice I might teach others also, than ten thousand words in an unknown tongue." (1 Cor. 14:19) God would not go to all the trouble of designing the gift of tongues for prayer and edification for the believer if it were not beneficial and to be put to use by the Christian. As Paul makes clear, he is very grateful that he can use this gift, and from his statement, he used it often.

Paul also makes clear that he was as comfortable with the manifestation of the Holy Spirit through tongues as he was with his own language. For he says in 1 Cor. 14:15, "I will pray with the spirit, and I will pray with the understanding also: I will sing with the spirit, and I will sing with the understanding also." God seeks to make the believer today as comfortable as Paul with the things of the Spirit.

While the intent of 1 Corinthians Chapter 14 is often misrepresented to discourage tongues, it is clear that its purpose was to set in order the proper and mature use of the gifts of the Spirit; for Paul admonished the Corinthians, "Brethren, be not children in understanding: howbeit in malice be ye children, but in understanding be men." (1 Cor. 14:20) Paul does not discourage the use of the gifts of the Spirit, but rather is establishing a decent order of things when the believers gather together. We know Paul advocated speaking in tongues and the baptism of the Holy Ghost, for we read of him in Acts 19:2, "And finding certain disciples, he said unto them, have ye received the Holy Ghost since ye believed? And they said unto him, we have not so much as heard whether there be any Holy Ghost ... And when Paul had laid his hands upon them, the Holy Ghost came on them; and they spake with tongues and prophesied." Paul didn't stop them and require an interpretation, for they were receiving their prayer language from the Spirit. Paul encourages prayer in the Spirit, for we read in Eph. 6:18, "Praying always with all prayer and supplication in the Spirit." Here, Paul does not state to pray with the understanding but in the Spirit, and he knew the difference, for he spoke clearly to that subject as we saw in 1 Cor. 14. The more one exercises the gift of praying in tongues, the more comfortable one feels with this manifestation of God's Spirit, and the more the Spirit can edify the individual. While one may be initially uncomfortable with this type of prayer, it should not be abandoned, for its foundation is in the word of God.

Another area where the believer needs regular experience before he can feel comfortable is praise and worship in private devotion. While it is relatively easy to worship with a group when others are doing likewise, when alone, many Christians feel uncomfortable in praising God. The Lord wants us to feel comfortable in His presence in praise and worship, but this takes practice. We are encouraged by scripture to praise God continually and are shown that there is indeed power in praise. We read in 2 Chron. 20:22, "And when they began to sing and to praise, the Lord set ambushments against the children which were come against Judah, and they were smitten." Often our comfort and strength come from God, not by laboring over a problem in prayer, but in praise. The Christian needs to learn to lift his voice in praise and song unto the Lord in private devotion even more than in gatherings of believers. We need not hesitate to enter God's presence to praise, for we are encouraged by God to do so. Heb. 10: 19 states, "Having therefore, brethren, boldness to enter into the holiest by the blood of Jesus." The believer's personal, private prayer life inwardly unites him with God. This union must be strong and continual in order for God to accomplish His work through the Christian.

The Principles of the Doctrine of Christ

Do you sometimes feel off balance in your walk with the Lord? Do you feel confused, or find you can become easily confused about God and your relationship with Him? Do you wish for a more stable walk with Him, and more confidence in your daily life in all of life's challenges? Then maybe a review of the basic foundational subjects of the Christian faith can help.

In the prior chapters, several subjects have been discussed in a sequence which brought forth God's intention for the believer through the inner working of the Holy Spirit. We spoke of the death of self, or the old nature flesh. This brought into focus the fact that God is working to strengthen the inner spiritual person while the old person of flesh is brought into subjection to the man of the spirit. Paul's words, "I die daily," (1 Cor. 15:31) take on substantial meaning in the process of inner spiritual growth as the flesh is put to death. We also spoke about the dangers of carnal interpretation of God's word. Studying and searching the word is essential. However, God clearly pointed out the error of taking the word and interpreting it outside of the light of the living Holy Spirit of God. We saw that God's purpose in feeding us with His word was not to solely educate the mind, but rather to transform the life of the believer into the likeness of Christ. We saw how unbelief was the tool of Satan to keep the power of the life of God out of the Church today, and that our carnal mind was quick to interpret scripture when unbelief was present in the heart.

We also saw God's goal for the Christian, which was to manifest God through the life lived. Even as the scripture says, "unto the stature of the fullness of Christ." (Eph. 4: 13) Jesus foretold of mighty works being accomplished through the believer by the power of the Holy Spirit, and that God desired to manifest not only the fruit of the Spirit, but also the power of the Spirit. We spoke on the need for the personal prayer life of the Christian to be proper before God could manifest Himself in the life. We learned that God sought to make the Christian feel comfortable with the things of the Spirit and ministry of the Holy Ghost. This was true in the private devotional life as well as the moving of the Spirit in a gathering of believers. We saw how the things of the Spirit indeed seemed foolish to the natural mind, and that God desired us to overcome this through the understanding of His word. It is important to take a Scriptural stand on such things as prayer and speaking in tongues, the baptism of the Holy Ghost, and the ministry of the laying on of hands for God has ordained all of these as manifestations of His Spirit.

Not only does the Lord desire us to understand where we are going in Him and what He desires to do with us, but it is also important that the basic foundations of the Christian faith be properly laid. In this chapter we will discuss the foundational truths from which Paul says we should go forward; but before going forward, we should be sure that these are in place according to God's word.

Paul describes the basics of the Christian faith in Hebrews 6:1. While Paul is admonishing them to go forward from these basics, we need to look at those things which he had already laid through the ministry of the Spirit as part of the principles, or commencement, or beginnings of their faith. We read, "Therefore leaving the principles of the doctrine of Christ let us go on unto perfection; not laying again the foundation of repentance from dead works, and of faith toward God, of the doctrine of baptisms, and of laying on of hands, and of resurrection of the dead, and of eternal judgment." (Hebrews 6:1-2) We will look briefly at each of these which Paul mentions above.

Repentance from dead works is the next principle. (Hebrews 6:1) The fundamental beginning of being a Christian is understanding that acceptance with God comes not by works of goodness or from abstaining from evil of itself. Acceptance with God comes as a gift given from God to the sinner as that person acknowledges what God has done through Jesus to save them. We are saved by grace through faith (Eph. 2:8), and our works have nothing to do with it. If one could attain righteousness through works, then Jesus died in vain, and the blood of the covenant which was shed on the cross is of no effect. This principle is vital, not only to salvation, but also to the Christian's walk in the Lord; for having begun by faith, we must realize that although works follow, works do not make us righteous. Our service for the Lord is not accepted in the sight of God because we are perfect and sinless, but rather because we know we are sinful and trust in His righteousness. This is true no matter what God is able to accomplish through a Christian. Pride, in self, develops rapidly if works are looked at as making us worthy in the sight of God. Thus, the truth of grace through faith, rather than dead works, is essential to a proper walk with the Lord. Paul speaks to this issue in Galatians 3 where he says, "Having begun in the Spirit, are ye now made perfect by the flesh? He that ministereth to you the Spirit, and worketh miracles among you, doeth he it by the works of the law, or by the hearing of faith?" (Gal. 3:3-5) Our faith is to be in God, not our good works nor our self-righteousness because of abstention from evil. Self-righteousness is as sinful in the sight of God as stealing or any other sin. God will keep us from evil as we stay near Him by His power, not by our good works.

Faith is coupled with repentance from dead works, for the foundation of Christ is laid in the heart of the believer as he exercises faith in God and His word. scripture tells us to have faith in Jesus; and when we repent of our sin and receive Him as Savior, we are born again, and the primary foundation is laid within our hearts. (1 Cor. 3:11) John 1:12-13 states, "But as many as received Him, to them gave He power to become sons of God, even to them that believe on His name: who were born, not of blood nor of flesh, nor of the will of man, but of God." Our foundation of acceptance by God is not a matter of having our name on a church roll, but rather of being born of God, through faith in Jesus. While salvation is an inner heart experience, the Lord requires that we confess Him before others. This confession of our faith solidifies our foundation even more. We read in Luke 12:8-9, "Whosoever shall confess me before men, him shall the son of man also confess before the angels of God: but he that denieth me before men shall be denied before the angels of God."

It is also important to understand that the foundation of salvation by faith is eternal. One cannot be born of God today, and tomorrow be bound for hell. If we sin, we do not become "unborn of God" and again in need of rebirth. The Bible is very clear that there are some vessels unto honor and some to dishonor, as well as some men's works being burned, yet they themselves being saved. (1 Cor. 3:15) As we understand the two natures in the Christian, the one born of God and the one of flesh, we can clearly see that if we allow the flesh and sin to reign in our bodies, then our reward will be small, and the account we give before the Lord will be shameful. However, our foundation by faith through grace is sure and in the hands of God. Works, whether good or bad, do not affect salvation. They may affect our reward and the words our Lord will speak to us when we stand to give an account of "those things done in our body." (2 Cor. 5:10) but they do not affect our salvation.

The principle of faith toward God is a daily principle. It must be exercised in the good times as well as the bad. If our foundation is shaky, in the times of testing, we might feel that God has left us, or perhaps we have lost our salvation. This is not true. scripture tells us, "Many are the afflictions of the righteous: but the Lord delivereth him out of them all." (Psalm 14:19) Peter admonishes us, "Beloved, think it not strange concerning the fiery trial which is to try you." (I Peter 4:12) Note that it is not the sinful who are in the fiery trial, but rather the beloved. We must not let outer circumstances shake our foundation. We can stand solidly upon the Lord and His word and know in all situations that "I am His and He has promised, He will never leave me nor forsake me!" (See Hebrews 13:5.)

The next principle mentioned by Paul is the doctrine of baptisms. This is plural and relates to the two baptisms for the New Testament Church. One is the baptism of water. This is done by the believer in obedience to the Lord's word. It symbolizes the death of the old nature and being raised again in newness of life with Christ. (Col. 2:12) The second is the baptism of the Holy Ghost. A clear scripture passage on this subject is found in Acts 8, where Peter and John prayed for certain believers to receive the Holy Ghost. The fact that the baptism of the Holy Spirit is a second experience following salvation is made clear in this story. Those receiving the Holy Spirit were already believers who had been baptized in the name of Jesus. Whether the baptism of the Holy Spirit comes simultaneously with salvation or separately, it is a needed equipping for the Christian. "Now when the apostles which were at Jerusalem heard that Samaria had received the word of God, they sent unto them Peter and John: who, when they were come down, prayed for them, that they might receive the Holy Ghost: (For as yet he was fallen upon none of them: only they were baptized in the name of the Lord Jesus.) Then laid they their hands on them, and they received the Holy Ghost." (Acts 8:14-17) In acts 19 we see another example of the baptism of the Holy Spirit as Paul prays for certain disciples in Ephesus. "And it came to pass, that while Apollos was at Corinth, Paul having passed through the upper coasts came to Ephesus: and finding certain disciples, he said unto them, have ye received the Holy Ghost since ye believed? And they said unto him, we have not so much as heard whether there be any Holy Ghost. And he said unto them, unto what then were ye baptized? And they said, unto John's baptism. Then said Paul, John verily baptized with the baptism of repentance, saying unto the people, that they should believe on him which should come after him, that is on Christ Jesus. When they heard this, they were baptized in the name of the Lord Jesus. And when Paul had laid his hands upon them, the Holy Ghost came on them: and they spake with tongues, and prophesied." (Acts 19: 1-6)

Paul did not teach that the baptism of the Holy Ghost was optional for the Christian. He placed it in the foundation section of his doctrine and instructed them to go forward, having these foundational truths laid in their hearts. scripture says the believers would receive power *after* the Holy Ghost was come upon them. The Christian today needs the baptism of the Holy Ghost as much as the apostles. We need to learn to be comfortable with the foundational truths of Christianity. Then we can go forward with a secure footing, not easily shaken. Neither water baptism nor the baptism of the Holy Ghost save us, but are fundamental elements of our faith.

The next principle is that of the laying on of hands. God has ordained the laying on of hands as a way in which the Holy Ghost will minister. In Acts 19 we read of how the Holy Ghost was given through the laying on of hands. In Acts 6 we see this principle in operation to pray for those who were called to serve the Lord. In First Timothy, we read of how Timothy apparently received gifts of the Spirit through the laying on of hands. In Acts 28 we see God healing through the laying on of hands, "And it came to pass that the father of Publius lay sick of a fever and of a bloody flux; to whom Paul entered in and prayed, and laid his hands on him, and healed him." (Acts 28:8) Paul was not healing, for hands of flesh cannot heal; but rather the ministry of the Holy Ghost was active, as God had ordained, through the laying on of hands. Jesus spoke of the believer saying, "They shall lay hands on the sick and they shall recover." (Mark 16:18) God has chosen to use His people as instruments of His hand, His healing, and His power. God honors the faith of the believer who moves in faith in what God ordains.

The next principle is the resurrection of the dead. The scripture states in John 5:28-29, "Marvel not at this; for the hour is coming, in which all that are in the graves shall hear his voice, and shall come forth; they that have done good, unto the resurrection of life; and they that have done evil unto the resurrection of damnation." It is important to realize that the grave is not the end for anyone. Every person will be resurrected to be judged by God. If we confess the Lord Jesus and receive Him as our Savior before we die, then we will be resurrected to eternal life. If we do not receive the Lord as Savior before we die, then we will be resurrected to eternal punishment. There is no opportunity to change our decision after death.

The last foundational truth mentioned here by Paul is that of eternal judgment. This relates to what is said concerning the resurrection. If our sins have not been cleansed by the blood of Jesus, and we do not know Him as Savior, then we are judged as guilty of sin and worthy of eternal torment. The Bible says, "It is appointed unto men once to die, but after this the judgment." (Hebrews 9:27) While the believer is not judged worthy of eternal punishment, he does not completely escape the judgment of God. The Bible tells us that we will all give account of ourselves before God. We do well to pay attention to the Lord today, so that we will not be ashamed before Him. As we read in 1 John 2:28, "And now, little children, abide in him; that when he shall appear, we may have confidence, and not be ashamed before him at his coming." Paul also strived to live pleasing unto the Lord, knowing full well the reality of the account he would give of his life. 2 Cor. 5:9-11, "Wherefore we labor, that whether present or absent, we may be accepted of Him. For we must all appear before the judgment seat of Christ; that everyone may receive the things done in his body, according to that he hath done, whether it be good or bad. Knowing therefore the terror of the Lord we persuade men."

To have a Scriptural understanding of the judgment only adds greater determination to press on with Jesus, that the account of our life might be pleasing in His sight. It is often easy to put off until later what we should be doing today regarding our walk with the Lord. However, to have these principles of Christianity made real to us by the Spirit of God, and to have our foundation in proper order, helps us live each day with the proper attitude. From these fundamentals, the Spirit of God bids us continue unto perfection; unto the fullness of the stature of Christ-God manifest in and through the lives of His people.

If Any Man Will Do His Will, He Shall Know

John 7:17

Many are the interpretations of God's word. God wants you to have faith in His word. But to have faith in the correct interpretation of His word requires that the light of your understanding come from His Spirit. He desires that you have clear understanding of His word; and it is for that reason He shows you the way to know of the doctrine, whether it be of Him or not. Though it may have seemed hidden, the key to pure understanding is not in the volume of your study alone, nor from a diversity of opinions meshed as one broadened view, rather the key is your will. Yes, and even more, your heart attitude. For it is written, "The pure in heart shall see God." (Matt. 5:8) For those whose hearts are cleansed from selfish ways and who desire to please only the Lord shall indeed be given the pure and correct understanding of His word.

Your cup cannot be filled with spiritual understanding of His word and, at the same time, be full of self-will. Truth does not abide in your mind alone but becomes a living reality in the chambers of your heart. For this reason, the pure knowledge of His word cannot occupy the same place as the ugliness of a selfish heart. He is the word, and in Him are all the treasures of knowledge and wisdom. Only as He is enthroned upon your heart will there be a revealing of truth by His Spirit. He will step aside if you choose to live for self rather than doing His will. How then do you think you will receive His understanding from the Holy Spirit if you shove Him out of your heart, for it abides with him? He will not force His will upon you.

As the Jews of old reasoned among themselves as to whether to believe His words or not, it was told them that they would never be able to know if the words Jesus spoke were of God until they did the will of God from the heart. While the mind of an individual can be filled with the letter of the word, spiritual understanding comes as the will of that individual is surrendered to the will of God. Service for God which is born of the will of an individual is not what God desires. He desires your service to be acceptable unto Him, and only as service is born of His life lived through you is God pleased. Many there are who serve God unacceptably, and He would not have you follow their error. (Matt. 7: 21-23)

Many are the religious vehicles which allow one to appear to serve God continually, but the Lord looks not upon the outer activities, but upon the heart. He knows if the life is laid down to do His will; or if a person, in his own power and will, is seeking to work for God. The only way you will find your eyes open to discern the difference is to lose your life. Lay down your will and allow Jesus to direct you daily. (Matt. 10:38-39) He brings you through many things which often seem useless and of no value in serving Him. He knows your opinion of these matters and cautions you to understand that His ways are not your ways. In every situation which crosses your will, the Lord enlarges your heart to receive more of Him; and His understanding comes with Him. If you want your own way in the smaller things of daily life and will not yield them up to God's control, you cannot receive the fullness of understanding. The Holy Spirit is working within you to help you understand; yet how can

He give you of more of Himself when you insist upon your own way? Learn to die to yourself through the common things of daily life, and you will find your ministry blossoming as God abides more and more within the space vacated as self-will is removed. God moves quickly to fill the void as you release to His control each portion of your heart and life.

Each person in your life, and every circumstance in which you find yourself, is a tool in God's hand for your eternal good and the good of others. Learn to yield to His refining, and be not of a questioning mind concerning the tools which He uses to accomplish His good work within your heart. As He brings you through trying situations, be not discouraged; for in these times, you will see yourself as you truly are, without righteousness and sinful. This is why Paul proclaimed, "Oh wretched man that I am." (Romans 7:24) God's Spirit was purging out the old to make room for the new. Rejoice in His presence in your life and stay near to Him with a repentant heart. Rebel not against that which comes to cross your will, for in each moment of death to self, you can be assured of a greater realization of the Lord's abiding presence. Hold tight to the work of the cross within your heart; for by doing so, you will surely see and know as He reveals truth to your heart by His Spirit. The Holy Spirit is the teacher, and He will give the correct light on the word.

Freedom vs. Folly

In today's world, it is easy to be persuaded. It is easy to put folks up on a pedestal and accept what they say without investigating what is going on in the spirit realm. Do we accept what someone says simply because they are popular and well accepted? Don't even these folks make mistakes and sometimes get into trouble? Should we follow them into trouble and deception, or work to pray about what we hear and seek God's opinion foremost?

Jesus said, "If the son therefore shall make you free, ye shall be free indeed." (John 8:36) God does not desire any person to be in bondage. To be set free by God is important and essential before the proper relationship can develop with God. If a person is yet in bondage, then the relationship of this person to the Father is not complete. There are many areas of life in which Jesus seeks to free a person; but for this writing, we will look at the freedom from other people and from outward religious forms and organizations. Not only must we understand our freedom, but it is also necessary that we understand some of the dangers which accompany freedom. Not that we are to fear freedom, but rather that we might have understanding concerning some of the pitfalls along the walk in the Spirit.

If the believer is fascinated with or trusting in a person or religious body, he must be freed for the proper development of his relationship with God to take place. In 1 Corinthians 3:4-9, when the believers began to associate themselves with the various persons ministering to them, Paul moved quickly to break their associating with the people and help them to associate with God their Father. We read, "For while one saith, I am of Paul, and another, I am of Apollos; are you not carnal? Who then is Paul, and who is Apollos, but ministers by whom ye believed, even as the Lord gave to every man? I have planted, Apollos watered; but God gave the increase. So then neither is he that planteth anything, neither he that watereth; but God that giveth the increase. Now he that planteth and he that watereth are one: and every man shall receive his own reward according to his own labour. For we are labourers together with God: ye are God's husbandry, ye are God's building." (1 Corinthians 3:4-9) Paul explains clearly that their identity is with God and not the various men used of God to minister to them. In 1 Corinthians 3:21 Paul states, "Therefore let no man glory in men," especially those used of God to minister. Paul's conclusion in 1 Corinthians 3:23 puts the individual's relationship with God in proper order by saying, "Ye are Christ's; and Christ is God's." While Paul taught the believers to associate with God and to break their fascination with the various people used of God, this same principle holds true when associating with any outer religious organization or group. Religions will perish. Denominations will be nonexistent in heaven and are nonexistent now in the Spirit. It is the individual's relationship with God that must be nourished, not his association with things in the outer.

The associating with men or things in the outer which began in 1 Corinthians 3 is yet prevalent today. The result is people attempting to bring others into their particular denomination or group rather than people preaching freedom from association with things in the outer and encouraging the individual to live properly in the eyes of God. The flow of the Spirit is from God to others, to cause others to know God, not join a group in the outer. While groups will of necessity form as gatherings of believers, the association is to be with Christ in the Spirit, not with the outer group or leader. As groups gather for fellowship, the gifts and ministries of the Spirit will be active to one degree or another. Also, people will be raised up by God to teach, preach, and minister to others. The danger is in our becoming fascinated with the fellowship group or people, in particular, as they are used of God. This is dangerous because we then begin to trust everything a person or group may do without testing the spirit and comparing it with the word of God. When there is fascination with people, discernment is not active.

Today, many are taught to trust people in positions of authority in Christianity because of religious training or because they are part of an accepted religious organization. We easily accept titles and positions without trying the spirit. We must be free from fascination with titles, religious positions, and organizations so that we can determine whether a person is moving in the Spirit. The thing that Christians must be taught to look for and recognize is the *anointing of the holy spirit*. If the Spirit is not bearing witness with the person or group, then positions, titles, and belonging to an accepted religious organization is vanity. God has removed His anointing from great people in the past, and only as we remain free from fascination with positions can we look for and trust in the anointing of the Spirit.

Deception is everywhere. To keep from being deceived, the Christian must learn to look for God's spiritual anointing, realizing that in the sight of God a person's heart attitude is what counts, not their degrees and/or titles. (God has used many a sheep herdsman when the heart of those in religious positions was not right.)

The proper flow of ministry is to help take the individual's eyes off the outer and direct our attention to God. The fascination in the outer must be broken through teaching and the work of the Spirit to free the individual from bondage to outer forms and people, and to encourage and nourish the individual in his relationship with God.

God desires to fill the believer with the power of His Spirit. If an individual looks to other individuals or groups in place of God personally, then this relationship cannot be fully established. We rob others of their full potential in Christ if we allow them to be fascinated with anything except Jesus.

While Paul taught freedom from association with humans, he also taught submission to the work of God through people. In Hebrews 13: 7-17 we read, "Remember them which have the rule over you, who have spoken unto you the word of God: whose faith follow, considering the end of their conversation ... Obey them that have the rule over you, and submit yourselves: for they watch for your souls, as they that must give account, that they may do it with joy, and not with grief." Yet this submission is not to be to the will of another person, but to the work of the Spirit through others. This always honors and respects each person's freedom in the Lord.

Once a person understands his complete freedom from others and his freedom from outer religious groups, there is the danger of the misuse of this truth. One can say, "I don't need other people, nor fellowship, for I am free, and Jesus is my teacher." While it is important not to gather where false doctrine is taught, the Bible clearly admonishes us to not forsake the assembling of ourselves together. (Heb. 10:25) Because freedom from humanness was taught by Paul, it was also necessary to teach the need to gather. A rebellious heart can misuse the truth of freedom to say, "I don't submit to any person to receive teaching or instruction." The Bible states in James 4:7, "Submit yourselves therefore to God." And it is God who chose to minister to people by placing other people into the ministry as described in Ephesians 4:11, "And he gave some, apostles; and some, prophets; and some, evangelists; and some, pastors and teachers." To refuse to submit to the teaching and instruction of the Spirit through other people is rebellion against God. (This does not mean to submit to a religious position or title, but to the anointing of the Holy Spirit.) The key to proper submission is freedom. Until a person is free from other individuals and outer groups, that person cannot try the spirits to assure they are of God. Once free, submission is proper, as long as freedom is retained and taught by those in overseer positions. Where there is fascination with people or religions, there is room for deception, and one person can lead many down the wrong path.

When we associate with a group in the outer, we feel God is pleased when we perform within this group to an accepted level of participation. We assume that if we attend all or most gatherings, then God will be pleased. This touches only a small portion of an individual's life. What about all of the time away from the gatherings? When freedom is preached, the individual is aware of a responsibility to always walk pleasing to God, not only in gatherings of believers. One can appear as a faithful and good Christian to many, and yet be full of much darkness in other areas of their life. A walk with God must be in the sight of the Lord and not in the sight of other people, for God looks upon the heart. Obedience is to be to God, moment by moment in all of one's life; and only as one associates with God directly does the whole life come under the light of the Spirit. Service in front of others is empty and hypocritical when the rest of the life is not right with God. (Isaiah 1:10-20) When one identifies with outer structures of religious activity, it is easy to justify some sin because of the other good things that one does. Such justification is compromise in the sight of God and not acceptable to Him. Such reasoning produces a goodness much like that spoken of by the prophet Hosea in Hosea 6:4, "For your goodness is as a morning cloud, and as the early dew it goeth away." While for a moment one can appear good in the eyes of others, yet the goodness can quickly fade if in the private life God is not allowed to transform, cleanse, and renew the heart and mind. We must identify with God the Father every moment in order for this proper transformation to happen. To properly identify with the Father, our fascination and identification with a person or outer groups must be broken and put in proper perspective. Attending fellowship meetings in no way substitutes for obedience to God with all the heart and life.

Anyone can often go in and out of fellowship meetings and be viewed by people as good. Yet only as the individual continually walks in the light of God will the life be pleasing to God. A person can smile, shake hands, and say, "Praise the Lord," in daily gatherings of believers. Yet if the private life is full of anger, hatred, and bitterness, such a person is missing a full relationship with God. While every person is a hypocrite to some degree, it is the work of the Spirit to eliminate hypocrisy and control every moment of the life. It is folly to misuse the truth of freedom, and folly to hide our sin under any amount of Christian activity. God desires a pure heart. (Heb. 4:13)

Except a Corn of Wheat Die

John 12:24

There is no way around it. If we want to walk with the Lord and get closer to Him, things in our lives and hearts will change. He will work on our inner self to change our hearts, to free us from our old ways and make us new. And sometimes that will hurt! Jesus tells us in John 12:24, "Verily, verily, I say unto you, except a corn of wheat fall into the ground and die, it abideth alone: but if it die it bringeth forth much fruit." Clearly death is a requirement for new life. Truly there could have been no resurrection had there first not been the crucifixion and death upon the cross. The principle Jesus is speaking of is vital to proper growth in our walk with the Lord. The cross stands for death, and when Jesus commands us to take up our cross and follow Him, it is a command to die to the old person and enter new life in Him. Too often the message of the cross is bypassed and not kept central to the gospel. To avoid the message of the cross and death to self is to miss the narrow gate of entrance into true spiritual light and understanding. Religion becomes appealing to the self-seeking when it speaks only of the promises and blessings, but leaves out the fundamental truth of death to the selfish old nature. One can speak from the word and use the correct terms of Christianity;

yet if the message attracts those who have "itching ears" (2 Tim. 4:3) desiring to live in self, the cross is not being preached.

The Bible warns us that people will turn away from the truth for a message which pleases them and requires no yielding of the will to God. Two Timothy 4:3 states, "For the time will come when they will not endure sound doctrine; but after their own lusts shall they heap to themselves teachers, having itching ears." To endure sound doctrine requires us to change, to give up the old and allow God to cross our will to mold us into His image. Truth is light and light reveals our willfulness, sin, rebellion, and error; to remain in the light requires repentance, humbleness and death to self. If we refuse to change and yield to the light of the truth, we become as those spoken of in 2 Timothy which will say, "No thank you," to the message of the cross and proceed to find a less convicting message. In many churches, the Gospel has become so watered down that it has lost its power to set people free from sin and self. It has allowed a person to feel comfortable in the dimly represented presence of God while being yet unclean, rebellious, and bound with sin and darkness. Holiness is forsaken for contemporary standards of living to keep pace with our modern sinful society. Darkness is accepted and fills many a heart because the light of truth which is brought forth is not the pure light of God's Spirit, but rather a shadow of religious teaching from the self-filled hearts of people with no power to free from sin. All of this occurs because the cross is forsaken, or modified, to not offend. The cross has always offended and always will! Grave is our error if we think to portray a "Self-pleasing Jesus" and a cross which does not mean death. The beauty of the preaching of the cross is that it not only brings death to the old nature, but truly sets one free---free to experience a walk with the Lord which is full of His resurrection power.

Progress in the Spirit is two-fold: one being the blessing of a greater partaking of God's Spirit, and the other being death to self. It is so easy to get excited over the gifts of the Spirit, experiences with the Lord, and God's indwelling Spirit expressing through us that the balancing factor of death is forgotten. To study, learn of God, and believe God for the moving of His Spirit in others and in ourselves is not necessarily the hard part. The hard part is the accompanying need to die. The proper expression of God's Spirit through the believer cannot take place until the will has come under the control of God. This requires death to self. If the things of the Spirit are sought without the inner work of death, then a person, in his own power, becomes the moving force behind the apparent gifts of the Spirit, and the flesh becomes the imitator of God. God never intended us to copy the expression of the Spirit, but rather become an empty vessel, yielded to God as an instrument of His Spirit. While the appearance is similar, the difference is great. Many people minister from the power of their own intellect rather than under the anointing of the Spirit of God. It is no wonder that we do not see the power of God manifest with signs and wonders; for He is not given control through death to self but is spoken of by those yet full of self, though possessing a knowledge of God's word.

A corn seed brings forth corn. A seed of wheat brings forth wheat. So it is that unyielded people bring forth unyielding Christians; and people-pleasing preachers speaking a cross which does not offend, bring forth and attract those having itching ears. It is easy to say, "I want to learn, but I don't want to yield or give up my own life." This type of learning does not bear fruit after the manner of the Spirit, but rather after the flesh. Our heart's cry should be, "I want to learn, and I want to yield control of my will to God." Then will knowledge be breathed upon by God's Spirit, and fruit will come forth from God. Teaching which brings forth the word without the message of the cross and death to self, is bringing forth only half of the message.

While we hear many eloquent speakers today, possessing a vast knowledge of the word, it is amazing how many speak against the things of the Spirit. The force behind them is their own intellect rather than the Spirit of God. We need to be cautious of what we accept. Many an impressive minister is impressive because of the charisma of his own personality or intellectual excellence. This does not mean he is anointed by God's Spirit. Only as the individual allows God to cross his will, yielding control to God, will he be able to discern the difference and not be deceived. While the scriptures admonish us not to judge our brother, God does not intend for His people to be ignorant and unable to discern between the flesh and the Spirit. To take an attitude of "everything is okay" because I am not to judge, is to accept blindness in place of sight and compromise in place of commitment to the light of God's truth.

God's work of the Spirit in the heart of each is accomplished in the common places of life. One does not need to seek great ways to sacrifice their life to die to self, but rather allow God to order the life. The Lord is a master at designing circumstances in the believer's life to accomplish the inner work of the Spirit in the heart. We find Jesus using our employment, the home, and every common chore of life. When cherished plans fall apart, God looks in the heart to see our reaction. When life does not bring us what we hoped for, God looks in the heart to see if we are desiring His will or our own. Until we yield to Him in the common things of life, we will not find the power of the Spirit active in us. The corn of wheat must die before it can bring forth fruit.

And He Shall Sit as a Refiner and Purifier of Silver

Malachi 3:3-4

God is going to work for us to get it right! He wants us to understand Him and see things clearly. He wants to remove the things in our hearts and lives that hinders our development in Him. Get ready to have your eyes opened as you seek Him with your whole heart! It is about the heart, not about what we do or don't do.

In Malachi 3:3-4 we read, "And he shall sit as a refiner and purifier of silver; and he shall purify the sons of Levi, and purge them as gold and silver, that they may offer unto the Lord an offering in righteousness. Then shall the offering of Judah and Jerusalem be pleasant unto the Lord." The book of Malachi is one of admonishment and rebuke to the people of God and the priests of that day. The people had not ceased from appearing to serve God (they were going through the motions), but they had strayed from the Lord in their hearts, and compromise had polluted their lives. The above scripture is God's answer to these people, saying ye must be purified first, before your offering will be pleasing unto Me. In chapter one we see that they had ceased to offer the best of their flock to the Lord, and yet they said, "What have we done wrong? We don't see where we have done wrong." Because their hearts were not right before God, and they were not totally yielded to Him, their compromise and sin was not visible to them. How sad it is when, because of our hardness of heart, we cannot see where we are wrong. Because of a polluted heart which seeks to serve God while pleasing self, we are blind to the pure way of the Spirit. It is no wonder that the Bible says, "He shall sit as a refiner and purifier." (Malachi 3:3) Truly this is the need today: that Jesus might be lifted up in holiness, not unrighteousness.

Isaiah cried out, "Who hath believed our report? And to whom is the arm of the Lord revealed?" (See Isaiah 53: 1) In Matt. 13: 14-15 we read, "And in them is fulfilled the prophecy of Esaias, which saith, by hearing ye shall hear, and shall not understand; and seeing ye shall see, and shall not perceive: for this peoples heart is waxed gross, and their ears are dull of hearing, and their eyes have they closed; lest at any time they should see with their eyes, and hear with their ears, and should understand with their heart and should be converted, and I should heal them." Many today have closed their eyes and ears to any message which would require change or giving up a portion of the life which is loved by self. As a result, we find that the witness of many is dimmed by the darkness of the flesh. The Jesus we profess is often represented by untransformed lives which, in ignorance, pollute His pure and holy image. Just as the priests in Malachi offered polluted sacrifices upon the altar, certain lives pollute their witness by mixing the ways of the flesh with the ways of the Spirit.

God is a God of holiness. He is a God to be feared with reverence and respect. He is not to be taken so lightly as to be fitted into our own personal life as we desire. We are to be transformed into His image. It is a grief to the heart of God when those who bear His name do not represent His holiness. We must ask ourselves if what we behold in much of the Christian world represents the Holy Son of God. Could we see Jesus fill the shoes of many who profess His name? Is the delivery of the message in accord with a Holy God? While there is much deception in that which appears to be religious, we must also not be deceived by that which mixes the world's ways with the Lord. Becoming all things to all people does not mean becoming fleshly and worldly to reach those at that level; nor does it mean clothing Jesus with the robes of the flesh to appeal to the fallen nature. It is the Holy Spirit which draws people unto Jesus, not our ingenuity. When the message of the Gospel is tailored to be comfortable for those loving the flesh, the response which results is not pleasing to the Lord. The priest's offerings were not pleasing to God in Malachi, nor are evangelical outreaches which are not born of the Holy Spirit of God.

When the Jesus which is lifted up is clothed with the darkness of the flesh, how can those who respond know in truth to whom they are responding? How can lives be transformed into His image when the image given is untransformed and polluted? God help us to give our lives totally unto Him that, as much as possible, we properly represent Him in this world. While multitudes may respond to a Jesus which is untransformed, we must remember we have been taught that the way to life is narrow, and the way is hard. The true way unto life is indeed hard because it requires a transformed life. A life which submits itself to the *refiner, the purifier*, becomes a new creature, not in word only, but in every aspect of one's life. It becomes a life which has been lifted up into the light of the Spirit, not a life which has pulled the things of God down to the level of the flesh. There is no portion of one's life which the Holy Spirit does not want to transform. He has purchased us with His blood, and it is the total man who He desires to transform. Thank God for His grace, understanding, and forgiveness, as He cleanses and purifies our hearts before Him. May we learn to yield to Him for His holy name's sake.

Go Ye into All the World and Preach the Gospel to Every Creature

Mark 16:15

Don't worry about rushing out to do many things for the Lord. It is best to wait for Him to send you. For Him to open the right doors at the right time. Works and activity for Him that are premature do more damage than good. Wait upon the Lord and resist the pressure to "do" before He leads you to.

The command which the Lord gave to His followers was clear. Yet it is misused and not always understood today. One may say, "How can one not understand such a straight-forward command?" We will look at how Jesus's command to His followers varies from how many interpret it today.

Jesus Himself spoke and told His disciples to go and preach. (Mark 16:15) It is still necessary today for Jesus Himself to speak to an individual heart in the same way in order for the going to preach to be initiated by God. Today in religion, we see people calling, pushing, and forcing others to go and preach, and making one feel guilty if he does not jump on the witnessing wagon. Then, in ignorance, the person has placed himself in charge of organizing the programs and filling the ranks of the workers. In many cases, babes are pushed into service because it is "doing for God" which is emphasized. Such emphasis is wrong. The way of the Spirit is never premature; and while His ways do not fit into the modern-day promotions of man, He is infinitely more effective through one vessel which is led of Him than one hundred which are prematurely pushed into service.

In Matthew 9:36-38 we read, "But when he saw the multitudes, he was moved with compassion on them, because they fainted, and were scattered abroad, as sheep having no shepherd. Then saith he unto his disciples, 'The harvest truly is plenteous, but the labourers are few; pray ye therefore the Lord of the harvest, that he will send forth labourers into his harvest." Jesus saw the great need for more workers, more preachers, and more followers to witness to the many people in need of God. It is beautiful how Jesus responded. He did not begin to enlist people to a witnessing campaign, nor to organize the sincerest of His followers to do the same. Instead, He says "Pray ye therefore the Lord of the harvest, that *He will send forth labourers into the harvest.*" (Matt. 9:38) Jesus knew that only God, through an inner work in the Spirit in one's heart, can prepare a person to go forth into the work of ministry in any capacity. Today, one sees the same need and does quite the opposite by promoting campaigns to prepare others to witness, teaching others how to lead souls to the Lord and how to be an effective Christian worker. While there is certainly nothing wrong with studying and seeking God for wisdom on how to be about His business, the emphasis is often totally wrong. While one places emphasis on getting others to work for God, the Spirit is moving to cause others to come and *know their god*. One can come through a course on how to witness for the Lord and have full confidence in the format he has been taught, but this does not mean that such a one *knows God*. One's trust should be in the ability of the Holy Spirit to draw others to Himself, not only in a four-step process to get others to accept the Lord. Jesus met each individual differently. Today the Spirit of God is no different. The truth is that when an individual's heart is close to God, and if a person knows the Lord and yields to Him in their daily life, the Spirit will use such a one to accomplish God's purpose and make them *His witness* through the Spirit. (While God may use all efforts to preach His word, He would have His people become dependent upon the Spirit and not a learned procedure.) God's way of putting people into service is far different and much more thorough than human's way. If God is dwelling in you, He will express Himself through you by the power of the Spirit, not because you have learned a format for being a "witness for the Lord." A person was never intended to be a "witness for the Lord," but rather God intends to witness to others Himself through the vessel of the believer by the power of the Holy Spirit.

There is a process through which the Spirit of God must take a believer to prepare him for service. This is not a school of evangelism as such, but rather a process of dying to self and yielding to God. As the life is yielded, the Spirit of God comes to increase the inner stature of the believer so that God can be manifest in the life and character of the individual. How foolish to think that one could be the Lord's witness by learning a procedure, while never yielding the life and heart to Him so that His character can be manifest as well as His written word. Because procedures and "getting involved" with religious activities have taken the place of yielding the heart and will to God, the power of God is absent from most of the Christian world today. It is easy to get into religious service. To get involved does not mean one is serving God in the Spirit. In fact, the Bible points out clearly that religious service will in no way get one into heaven unless it is born out of a relationship with Jesus. Again, this points to the need for the emphasis to be on getting to know the Lord by yielding the will to Him rather than on pushing others into service. Matthew 7:21-23 states "Not everyone that saith unto me, Lord, Lord, shall enter into the kingdom of heaven; but he that doeth the will of my Father which is in heaven. Many will say to me in that day, Lord,

Lord, have we not prophesied in thy name? and in thy name have cast out devils? and in thy name done many wonderful works? And then will I profess unto them, *I never knew you*: depart from me, ye that work iniquity." Jesus speaks plainly here, showing that all of the wonderful works one can do in religion are iniquity, unless they are initiated *by Him* out of a relationship with Him. Jesus is certainly capable of sending others into service by the Spirit, and man has no right to be sending those whom Jesus has not prepared and sent.

The process of yielding to God is where the emphasis must be, thus allowing God to accomplish the inner work necessary to give spiritual stature to His servants. Then God Himself will send them into the harvest with the power of the Spirit. One of the Bible's clearest examples of the Spirit's way of preparation is the story of David. (See 1 Sam. Chapter 16 through 2 Sam. Chapter 2.) Called of God and anointed by Samuel, the events of David's life that led to the eventual position of King are truly God's way of preparation. David's life took a course which seemed absolutely opposite of what one would expect. Instead of to the throne (or into service), David becomes a fugitive running for his life. Twice he could have slain Saul and taken the kingdom prematurely but did not. Much later God prepared the way for David to become King. Even then, it was not over the entire nation, but only over Judah. Later, the fullness of the original calling was brought to pass. Why was all of this necessary? Because through all the events of testing and waiting, God was building a kingly heart in David. A heart that would let God do the work in His way. Today, God must do the same inner work in the believer to assure that the Spirit can do the Spirit's work in His way, and not have man try and take control of ministry in self-will. This process of dying to self and learning God's way is perhaps the most difficult part of walking in the Spirit and is the most absent from much of Christianity. Man has designed programs and requirements to enter service which have little or nothing to do with the inner preparation of the Spirit in the heart of the individual. One can be a graduate of the finest seminary and yet never have yielded self-will to God or walked in the Spirit. Many pulpits are filled with men laden with degrees and religious titles and honors yet are babes in the Spirit with no true power or authority from God. They are the product of a religious process and not the process of the Spirit.

When scripture says go and preach, the intention is for you to go in power and under the anointing of the Holy Spirit. We read in Mark 16: 20, "And they went forth, and preached everywhere, *the Lord working with them, and confirming the word with signs following.*" He sent them because they were prepared and had the inner stature in the Spirit to go in the power of the Spirit, and God bore them witness. God never intended His ministers to not have power, but only those who are graduates of the Spirit's process will experience such a power and anointing. There is a clear example in Acts 19:13-16 of those who had the proper name and procedure, yet no power. They had no power because they had not been through the Spirit's process of dying to self and yielding to God in order to *know Him and His ways.* We read, "Then certain of the vagabond Jews, exorcists, took upon them to call over them which had evil spirits the name of the Lord Jesus, saying, we adjure you by Jesus whom Paul preacheth. And there were seven sons of one Sceva, a Jew, and chief of the priests, which did so. And the evil spirit answered and said, Jesus I know, and Paul I know; but who are ye? And the man in whom the evil spirit was leaped on them, and overcame them, and prevailed against them, so that they fled out of that house naked and wounded." (Acts 19:13-16) When the authority of God is in control, the demons flee...not the servants.

Only the Spirit of God can teach a person how to be His witness. Man cannot teach others how to preach, pray, witness, get the gifts or get the power. If men can be taught to yield to God and allow Him to lead them through the process of yielding, then God will manifest Himself to and through the believer. Paul puts it very accurately when he says, "I labour, striving according to his working, which worketh in me mightily." (Colossians 1:29) Paul was not working because he was taught by man or told to do so. He was working because God was working *in him*. The process of the Spirit which crucifies self was active in Paul, and as a result, the power of the Spirit was also active. Service which is activated by any source other than the Lord's working is of man or Satan and will not carry God's anointing with it. While religion offers positions of service and authority within the organized structure, only God can give spiritual authority and power.

Before you go and preach, yield your heart and life to Him. You need to go to the cross, go through the process of yielding to Him and learning His ways. Go through the Spirit's process of dying to self-will and giving His Spirit control of our life. Then, and only then, will you hear Jesus clearly when He does speak and send you out. And when He sends you, you will preach with His power and with His authority and with His anointing. for He has anointed you to preach the word. He will work with you and will confirm the word with the power of His Spirit. Will you give Him the depths of your heart and your desires that He might make you, His vessel? He has a way for you to walk which will prosper you and build you up in the Spirit. Will you trust Him as He takes you in the way? You cannot obtain the riches of His Spirit in any other way. Do not be deceived by much activity, for He has called you to walk in the Spirit's ways. Easy it is to be outwardly active and of good report, but the Lord requires you to sell all that you have and follow Him. The selling is that of the heart. Giving to Him the center of your will is the 'selling all' that must be done if you would be a partaker of the treasures of heaven. Even as He said to the rich young ruler, "Sell all that thou hast... and thou shalt have treasure in heaven." (Matt 19:21) the same is true for you today. You will surely have the riches of heaven bestowed upon you this day as you sell out, owning no more the control of your life. He does not call you to service; He calls you to sell all. Then, the Lord will minister through you.

The Devil Walketh About Seeking Whom He May Devour

1 Peter 5:8

Expect to be attacked in the spirit as you receive more of God's Spirit in your life. Don't be surprised by this. Be prepared.

Much has been said and written about the baptism of the Holy Spirit. There has been much criticism about the gift of tongues, emotionalism, and the misuse of the gifts. No amount of criticism, even if well-founded, should ever be allowed to take the gifts of the Spirit out of operation in the church today. Our warfare is on the battlefield of the Spirit, and we need the power of the Spirit to stand undefeated and fight against the powers of darkness. Jesus was clear in Acts 1:8 when He said, "Ye shall receive power after that the Holy Ghost is come upon you." Because this is true, Satan moves in any way he can to cut off the power which is a threat to his kingdom. It is Satan that moves men to speak against the baptism of the Holy Ghost and speaking in tongues. The scripture states that "He that speaketh in an unknown tongue edifieth himself." (1 Cor. 14:4) Satan is the one who doesn't want the believer to be edified.

Misuse should be revealed as such without destroying the purpose and divine intention behind the gifts. To use an old expression, "You don't throw out the baby with the bath water." There can be no question that those baptized with the Holy Ghost spoke with other tongues. Paul said, "I thank my God, I speak with tongues more than ye all." (1 Cor. 14:18) Today, the believer needs more than ever to be baptized with the Holy Spirit and speaking in tongues in his prayer life to overcome the powers of darkness.

Satan is subtle. If he can't keep us from believing in the baptism and the usefulness of praying in the Spirit (tongues), he will try and keep it from being preached and practiced in the fellowship. Carnal reasoning says, "Let's be reasonable lest we offend someone." While there is a definite Scriptural order to the gifts, it is Satan who would keep them hidden to where they cease being used. "Reasonableness" which leads to the quenching of the gifts of the Spirit is sin. If Satan can keep the baptism of the Holy Ghost and speaking in tongues from being talked about, soon those that have the gift stop using it and others who would have received are not told about it. And what has happened? Satan has stepped in with religious garments and "reasonable thinking" to keep the Spirit and His power out of the Church.

If a fellowship doesn't preach the baptism of the Holy Ghost and speaking in tongues, then Satan has entered to quench the moving of the Spirit of God. A closing thought: In 1 Corinthians 14:14-15, Paul states that praying in the Spirit is not praying with the understanding. How then is one to pray *in the spirit* as commanded in Ephesians 6:18 & Jude 20, if one doesn't pray in tongues?

Faith and Fire

In this chapter we will be looking at what we should expect as we receive by faith the word of God and seek to continue in what the Holy Spirit teaches. Satan is the enemy of truth and seeks to destroy our faith in the truth. If the believer is not taught what to expect as he begins to rejoice in the revelations of the Holy Spirit, much can be lost through the work of the devil. Jesus spoke of the parable of the sower, explaining several ways in which the truth which is sown in the heart can be destroyed or hindered (Matt. 13). In all three examples of the seeds of truth being hindered, Satan and the carnal fallen nature of man are the reasons. While each Christian must make his own decision to continue in the teaching of the Lord, it is helpful to know what to expect so that those who would desire to follow the way of the Lord are not side-tracked by the confusion of the evil one.

In Matthew 13:19 we read, "When any one heareth the word of the kingdom, and understandeth it not, then cometh the wicked one, and catcheth away that which was sown in his heart." Here we see the carnal mind, which cannot understand the things of the Lord, persuaded by the devil to forsake the truth heard because of a lack of understanding. (1 Cor. 2:14) In Matthew 13:22 we read, "He also that received seed among the thorns is he that heareth the word; and the care of this world, and the deceitfulness of riches, choke the word, and he becometh unfruitful."

Here again we see the tempter making the things of this life look extremely pleasing and to be sought after by appealing to man's fallen nature. This is the same tactic which the devil used on Jesus in Matthew chapter four. Being aware of how the devil seeks to destroy a man's faith in the word of God makes it more difficult for him to succeed. In the above examples, we are made aware of the danger of throwing away the seeds of truth because we do not find them always easy to understand. We must learn to leave with God those things we do not understand lest they be used against us. His light comes a little at a time as we are able to bear it. (John 16: 12-13) Peter gives the same warning in 2 Peter 3:16 when he speaks of some of Paul's writings saying, "As in all his epistles, speaking in them of these things; in which are some things hard to be understood, which they which are unlearned and unstable wrest, as they do also the other scriptures, unto their own destruction." Likewise, being aware of the devil's intention to make this world and the things in it appear glorious and worth our pursuit, we should have good reason to resist his lies. Jesus gives us this example in Matthew 4;8-10, "Again, the devil taketh him up into an exceeding high mountain, and sheweth him all the kingdoms of the world, and the glory of them; and saith unto him, 'all these things will I give thee if thou wilt fall down and worship me.' Then saith Jesus unto him, 'Get thee hence, Satan: for it is written, thou shalt worship the Lord thy God, and him only shalt thou serve." Our response should be the same!

The last of the three examples of evil seeking to destroy and rob a soul of truth, as told in the parable of the sower, is in Matthew 13:20-21, "But he that received the seed into stony places, the same is he that heareth the word, and anon with joy receiveth it; yet hath he not root in himself, but dureth for a while; for when tribulation or persecution ariseth because of the word, by and by he is offended." Here we see the devil causing others to come against the truth within the believer, and the believer forsaking truth because of the adversity it is causing. This scripture, perhaps more than the others, brings us to the theme of this article, that being *Faith and Fire*.

In a prior chapter we spoke of the communications link which

Jesus died to create between the believer and God the Father. Because of the work of the Holy Spirit, one today is enlightened by the Spirit of God as God makes us understand His word and quickens His truth to our hearts. It is in this quickened truth, given to us by God Himself that we are to place our faith. We must learn to trust in and cling to God's word more than any other thing. It is this faith in the quickened truth of God's word the devil is out to destroy. Satan hates the light of God's truth in the believer. The quickened truth of God is the devil's target. The parable of the sower gives us general insight into some of the ways which the devil seeks to destroy faith in the word of God. Now, let us be a bit more specific.

Fire can serve two purposes. It can refine, and it can destroy. We will first speak of the fire which destroys. James 3:5-6 gives a clear description of the fire which destroys; that being the tongue, or more clearly, words that are spoken. We read, "Even so the tongue is a little member, and boasteth great things. Behold how great a matter a little fire kindleth! And the *tongue is a fire*, a world of iniquity; so is the tongue among our members, that it defileth the whole body, and setteth on fire the course of nature; and it is set on fire of hell." (James 3:5-6) The tongue which is a destroying fire is the tongue which speaks against the truth of God's word. A Christian tongue which speaks from a position in the carnal mind, against the word, which is quickened by the Holy Spirit, is more destructive in nature than a lashing from an unbeliever. James warns against speaking with fleshly wisdom which is given from the devil. When the word of God is framed in the context of such evil wisdom, it becomes a fire which seeks to destroy the truth given by the Holy Spirit. James 3:14-15 states, "But if ye have bitter envying and strife in your hearts, glory not, and lie not against the truth. This wisdom decendeth not from above, but is earthly, sensual, devilish." Any teaching which opposes the things of the Spirit is born of this devilish wisdom.

When God quickens truth to the heart of the believer, it is likened unto a parchment scroll in the heart upon which God writes His quickened word. The tongue of the carnally minded is likened unto the flame of hell which seeks to burn up the scroll upon which this word is written. We must be aware and not surprised as the devil stirs up those around us to come against the truth which the Lord writes upon the heart. When the Lord places a seed of truth within the heart, the devil comes through the tongue of anyone he can to say, "You don't really understand it all anyway, throw it away. " (Matt. 13: 19) Or the devil will cause someone else to speak against you, mocking the truth you have received and persecuting you. Often the devil has others say that you are off the path and have listened to the devil yourself, even as they said of Jesus (Matt. 13:21 & John 8:48). Therefore, it is so critical that the believer be seeking God, believing in the communications channel which He established through the death of His Son and the sending of the Holy Spirit as our teacher. So often, when one is saved and begins to share his newfound understanding of Jesus, or is baptized in the Holy Ghost and receives the language of the Spirit, the fire of devilish wisdom seeks to destroy the truth and beauty of what God has given. Thank God that we have power over the evil one in the name of Jesus. Let us pray that we are not hindered in using it when the truth of God is being assailed in our hearts by the confusion of the devil.

The second purpose of fire is to refine. In Daniel chapter three, we read of the three Hebrews who were thrown into the fiery furnace. This furnace had two effects. It destroyed those who had thrown the three into the flames, and it refined the faith of those cast in. So, it is with the fire which comes to try our faith. 1 Peter 1:7 states, "That the trial of your faith, being much more precious than of gold that perisheth, though it be tried with fire, might be found unto praise and honour and glory at the appearing of Jesus Christ." The faith which is to be tried is faith in the word of God as the Holy Spirit gives us understanding.

The same fire which attempts to destroy the scroll within the heart, upon which God has quickened His word, is the fire which is used of God to refine our faith in that which the Lord has given.

Whether we are destroyed or refined by the flames depends upon us. If we obey the word and stand upon it, refusing to compromise the truth of the Lord, then we will be thrown into the *refining* fire, not the destroying fire. If we compromise to avoid adversity or please others, we allow Satan to place his fire on the edges of the scroll, and it begins to burn.

In Daniel 3:6 we read, "And whoso falleth not down and worshippeth shall the same hour be cast into the midst of a burning fiery furnace." This principle is still true today. For if we will not bow down to the pressure to compromise truth, or to forsake it, and if we do not yield to the pressure of carnal devilish wisdom, we will be thrown into the fire. However, as stated above, the fire we enter because of standing upon God's word is a refining fire. It will produce greater strength and greater faith in God and in the truth, we receive from the Holy Spirit. The Hebrews came out of the furnace without harm, and so can we. (Dan. 3:27.

God has purposed that all things will be tried by fire, and of a truth the trying has begun. The believer can expect to have his faith in the truth he receives subjected to all of the following: tested by the fire of carnal wisdom; challenged by loved ones who do not understand or agree; tested against religious tradition; challenged by carnally minded men in seemingly high religious positions; weighed for value against the riches of this world; tested by the fire of the tongue; threatened by his own self-will and flesh. And to what purpose? Faith that burns in the fire is not worthy of the Kingdom of God. God's intention is that our faith "be found unto praise and honour and glory at the appearing of Jesus Christ." (1 Peter 1:7)

Faith placed in the fire will either be burned or refined. God grant us the will to continue in the fullness of His glorious truth, and a refinable faith that trusts in the word of God and the Holy Spirit's power to open the understanding through the fieriest of testing, even unto death. "Fear none of those things which thou shalt suffer... be thou faithful unto death, and I will give thee a crown of life." Revelations 2:10

Now You Say, "We See," Therefore Your Sin Remaineth

John 9:41

By what light do we see and understand? Do we see by the light of God, or by some other light? What do we consider to be the light of God? These questions seem simple enough and with confidence most Christians would answer them. Perhaps this is exactly the greatest danger...confidence. Confidence which is not truly placed in God's word and Holy Spirit. It is subtle, but much of the Christian world teaches confidence in the religious system rather than confidence in God. One can be a shining product of a religious system while being far from the product of the Holy Spirit. The Pharisees had this very problem. They were the product of the religious system of the day, the very system which had been ordained by God. When Jesus, who was sent of the Spirit, came unto them, they felt they already knew everything correctly and had no room to receive what was of the Spirit. They had fallen into the trap of thinking that the religious system was light. They couldn't see anything wrong with themselves and thought they were truly seeing by the light of God. Jesus said of them in John 9:41, "But now ye say 'we see'; therefore, your sin remaineth." They were seeing by the wrong light and didn't know they were blind.

The laws and ordinances which God had set forth for Israel, had become empty of the Spirit of God and while on the outer the activities looked religious or godly, yet within the heart of many of the people there was darkness and not light. That is what Jesus was referencing when He said the religious leaders where like whited sepulchers, which looked good outwardly but inside were dead. (Matt. 23:27) Christian churches and denominations can have a similar problem. Having begun correctly, sometimes doctrine, rules and procedures take precedence over the things of the Spirit and then darkness and deadness prevail. They can make no room for the Holy Spirit but can look deeply religious and good on the outside.

Jesus warned of this very thing in Matt. 6:23, "If therefore the light that is in thee be darkness, how great is that darkness." When one is seeing by the true light of the Spirit, he is able to see who is in control, self or God. This is what the Pharisees missed. Being a graduate of a religious organization or being ordained by one does not mean God is in control. We are in great danger of being deceived when we look to the religious system as light and authority. While products of the religious system are given authority within the system, it does not mean they have been given authority from God. The Pharisees (who had authority in the system) asked Jesus (who had the authority of the Almighty), "By what authority doest thou these things? And who gave thee this authority?" (Matt. 21:23) Because they saw by the wrong light, they missed seeing that their own hearts were not right. The Lord knew that their hearts were not right for He called them blind leaders of the blind, and whited sepulchers, appearing holy unto men, yet inwardly full of wickedness. Throughout the ministry of the Lord Jesus, the products of the religious system spoke against Him. They said He was of the devil and could not be of God, because He did not fit into the system which they themselves had corrupted. In scripture we see a clear example of the ones full of self, looking to the one full of the Spirit and branding such a one rebellious and out of line; the ones seeing by the wrong light calling the true light darkness.

Jesus made a profound statement about how to see by the true light and not by a false light in John 7:17, "If any man will do His (God's) will, he shall know of the doctrine, whether it be of God, or whether I speak of Myself." The question of which light we see by becomes an issue of control. Who is in control of your life? Is self-will what we strive for, or God's will and the death to self? To see by the true light, one must give control of one's life to God. (Jesus is the true light.) In order to walk in the true light of Jesus, we must do as He said in Luke 9:23, "If any man will come after me, let him deny himself, and take up his cross daily, and follow Me." (Matt. 16:24) Knowledge, training, authority within the system schooling, and degrees can never become a substitute for death to self and yielding to God. The light by which we see is determined by where we stand. If we stand in darkness, we see through darkness. If we stand in the light, we see through the light. Jesus is the light, and to stand with Him requires yielding the will to God. There is no other way.

A Thought on The Barren, The Emotional, and The Spiritual

Depending upon where we are standing, we will view the moving of the Spirit differently. This relates to the light by which we see, the light of the Spirit of God, or the light of a religious system, or by some other light. There are three places we can be in relation to the moving of the Holy Spirit. One is to be barren. We can hold no place in our life or fellowship for such things as healing, miracles, prophecy, speaking in tongues, the baptism of the Holy Ghost, or the laying on of hands. Another position is emotionalism. Weeping may abound. Shouts of praise, prophecy, and tongues seem to have no order or control, and any outburst, regardless of how disruptive, is accepted as the moving of God's Spirit. Great effort is made to stir everyone up in the song and worship; but unfortunately, the results are great excitement about everyone getting excited, but not a true moving of God's Spirit.

Being barren or emotional as described above are equally incorrect. One thing to know is that the barren will call emotionalism and the true moving of the Spirit the same thing, emotional. Those who are emotional will call the barren, barren and are not aware that they themselves are not being spiritual. The place where God desires us to be is in the Spirit. Here, the Holy Spirit has control of the emotions. The moving of the Spirit is not disruptive. The gifts will operate as the hearts are yielded to Him. Those in this position in Christ will see the barren as they are, barren. They will see the emotional for what they are-somewhat out of control and a bit off from where God would have them. They also will suffer criticism from the barren, who will brand them as emotional fanatics; however, their rejoicing is great, for regardless of what anyone says, when you are in the Spirit, you see in the true light. Even as the blind man who had received his sight proclaimed, "One thing I know, that, whereas I was blind, now I see." John 9:25.

They Which Preach the Gospel, Should Live of The Gospel

1 Corinthians 9:14

The principle of tithing is nearly as old as the scriptures, beginning with Abraham and Jacob. We read of Jacob saying, "And of all that thou shalt give me I will surely give the tenth unto Thee." (Genesis 28:22) Thus, much of today's tithing is based upon a tenth of what we receive. As we read further into the New Testament, we see that as the Spirit moved men's hearts, they gave not a tenth, but truly all they had. Acts 2:44-45, "And all that believed were together, and had all things common and sold their possessions and goods and parted them to all men, as every man had need." Again, in Acts 4 we read of others selling their lands and houses and giving the money to the apostles who distributed to the others as they had need. Jesus taught a dedication to Him that was total, giving Him control of every aspect of the life, including one's finances. In Luke 14:33 Jesus said, "So likewise, whosoever he be of you that forsaketh not all that he hath, he cannot be My disciple." This is the attitude of heart that God desires us to have, giving all to His control.

God is clear that if we do not give of our substance to His work, we are robbing Him. He is equally encouraging by challenging the believer to give and see if God will not bless the giver abundantly. "Will a man rob God? Yet ye have robbed me. But ye say, wherein have we robbed Thee? In tithes and offerings. Ye are cursed with a curse, for ye have robbed Me, even this whole nation. Bring ye all the tithes into the storehouse, that there may be meat in Mine house, and prove Me now herewith, saith the Lord of hosts, if I will not open you the windows of Heaven, and pour you out a blessing, that there shall not be room enough to receive it." (Mal. 3:8-10) It takes faith to accept the Lord's challenge.

Giving is a sound Biblical principle; and because it is, it can be exploited to further the will of man. This relates to the prior chapter on control. If God is in control, man will not misuse the principle of giving to further his own plans for the Lord.

If a man or ministry must ask for financial support to keep going, somewhere they are ahead of the Lord, and such begging should be a warning sign that something is wrong. We must exercise great care in our giving, not to give to that which the Lord Himself has chosen not to support. The mere fact that it is a good cause is not reason enough to give God's money. We should give as led of the Lord and not be deceived by the sad practice which has been allowed to creep into the Faith. When ministries must make pleas to pay their bills, or build the next building, they have stepped ahead of Jesus, and this is no reason to help them. When God is in control, begging, in whatever form it comes, is not to be found. Paul put it well "If others be partakers of this power over you, are not we rather? Nevertheless, we have not used this power: but suffer all things, lest we should hinder the gospel of Christ ... What is my reward then? Verily, that when I preach the gospel, I may make the gospel of Christ without charge, that I abuse not my power in the gospel." (1 Cor. 9:12 & 18)

To live of the gospel goes much farther than looking to receive financial support. To live of the Gospel is to abide by and obey God's word fully, to live subject to the ways of the Spirit and to give God control. If God wants a ministry to continue, it will; and all the powers of hell can't stop it. No one has a right to expect to receive money from the Lord for ministry when they misuse the principle of giving in self-will for their own purposes, regardless of how good and religious those purposes may sound.

Israel Hath Sinned, Therefore They Could Not Stand Before Their Enemies

Joshua 7:11-12

God is all about what is in our hearts. And, if we have things in there that He wants to deal with, our lives can be very difficult until we listen to His still small voice and obey what He is trying to tell us. We can bring unnecessary problems into our lives, prolong a difficult season, and pay a heavy price if we do not listen to Him well.

In Joshua 7 we read of Israel's defeat in trying to overthrow the city of Ai because there was sin in the camp. God had just finished giving Israel a mighty victory in the taking of Jericho, and since Ai was much smaller, it seemed an easy victory. However, because God was displeased with one person in the congregation, He allowed the men of Ai to defeat the children of Israel. Sin was in the camp, but they were not aware of it. God then moved to call their attention to the fact that something was wrong, and He got their attention following their defeat at Ai. Often, we too march boldly along with victory and blessing on every side, having little need to examine our hearts before God, until our Ai comes along to cause us to stop and seek the face of the Lord. Truly the heart of the believer can be likened unto the camp and nation of Israel.

Joshua then humbles himself before the Lord with the elders of Israel and prays, "Alas, 0 Lord God, wherefore hast Thou at all brought this people over Jordan, to deliver us into the hand of the Amorites, to destroy us? Would to God we had been content, and dwelt on the other side of Jordan! 0h Lord, what shall I say, when Israel turneth their backs before their enemies! For the Canaanites and all the inhabitants of the land shall hear of it, and shall environ us round and cut off our name from the earth: and what wilt thou do unto thy great name?" (Joshua 7:7) At this point, all Joshua knew was that something was wrong. He didn't know what. God then told him in Joshua 7:10, "Get thee up; wherefore liest thou thus upon thy face? Israel hath sinned ...for they have even taken of the accursed thing, and have also stolen, and dissembled also, and they have put it even among their own stuff. Therefore, the children of Israel could not stand before their enemies, but turned their backs before their enemies." God then proceeded to root out the one who had sinned saying, "There is an accursed thing in the midst of thee, 0 Israel: thou canst not stand before thine enemies, until ye take away the accursed thing from among you. " (Joshua 7:13) Achan was then revealed as the one who had taken a Babylonish garment, and two hundred shekels of silver, and a wedge of gold of fifty shekels weight. Achan and all his family and possessions were then destroyed, and God again restored His blessing to Israel and gave them victory.

The story of Joshua and Ai can truly be likened unto the working of the Holy Spirit in the heart of the believer. It is the Holy Spirit that reveals truth and brings God's light into our hearts and our understanding. ("He will reprove the world of sin" John 16:8). There is a reason for God wanting to reveal sin in our hearts and remove it. Sin and bondage are partners, and God desires us to be free from the bondage that is the result of sin. Proverbs 5:22 states, "He shall be holden with the cords of his sins." Christ died to free us from the cords of our sins so that we might know the freedom of which He spoke. Jesus said, "Ye shall know the truth, and the truth shall make you free." (John 8:32) Just as God shined His light into the camp of Israel and pointed out the problem, so the Holy Spirit is desirous of doing the same in our hearts so that we might press on in our walk with the Lord. While Israel's defeat at Ai did not lead them into bondage, it would have resulted in bondage had the sin been allowed to remain. There would have been other defeats until God was allowed to remove the problem. This was Joshua's fear when he prayed, "For the Canaanites and all the inhabitants of the land shall hear of it, and shall environ us round, and cut off our name from the earth." (Joshua 7:9)

There is no area of the heart into which God does not desire to shine His light to expose sin and remove it. We have the choice of allowing God to reveal sin and remove it. We are wise if we allow him to do so. John 3:19-21 points out a need to be humble and desirous of being reproved by the Holy Spirit's light, "And this is the condemnation that light is come into the world, and men loved darkness rather than light, because their deeds were evil. For everyone that doeth evil hateth the light, neither cometh to the light, lest his deeds should be reproved. But he that doeth truth cometh to the light, that his deeds may be made manifest, that they are wrought in God."

If we cling to our own selfish ways and wants, even though we attempt to fortify them with scripture, we are only deceiving ourselves and remain in bondage to our own flesh. Such stubbornness is better termed rebellion. What is needed is submission to God's will and way for our life. Such proper submission will lead to the crossing of our will, even as we read of Jesus in Matthew 6:10, "And he went a little further, and fell on his face and prayed, saying, 'O my Father, if it be possible, let this cup pass from me: nevertheless, not as I will, but as thou wilt!" This type of submissive heart attitude leads to true freedom; for in the Lord's path for our life, events, circumstances, people, yes, everything-is planned to help rid our hearts of sin and free us into a greater relationship with Him. If we desire to be free, we must learn to submit to God's will and direction for our life. While there are many areas of our hearts to which God is desirous of bringing His light, one area of sin and bondage which is subtle and often hard to discern is that of false submission.

There is a danger in learning submission. The crossing of the will should not be confused with the giving of the will to anything except God. Often, those who fear rebellion and want no part of it can become easy candidates for bondage in the name of submission. It is sometimes easier to learn submission than it is to learn to take a stand in the Spirit. One fears to take a stand lest he be accused of being rebellious. Proper submission will take the soul of one full circle; from standing in rebellion to the crossing of the will; to submitting to the will of God; to learning to stand once again, only not in rebellion, but rather in the Spirit and light of the Lord. God does not want the soul captive by the strong wills of others, Christian or non-Christian. If we allow other people to have control of our will (even partial control) then we have been brought into bondage; and very possibly it has happened in the name of submission.

God helps us by several points in scripture to not become bound or controlled by others. Sin is the root cause of the cords of bondage. In false submission to our own self-will or the will of others, sin is the root problem. In a way, it relates to the sin of Achan, who coveted after the gold and silver. Achan allowed something other than the will and purpose of God to have access to his will; and the result was sin and ultimately death. While here it appears that Achan's own selfish desires were the things to which he submitted, it could have been his wife or children who urged him to bring back some treasure from the spoil.

If we place the desires of others above the desires of the Lord, we sin, and the result is bondage; sometimes to the will of another and sometimes to the will of the old flesh man. Christ died to free us from the bondage of having our will controlled by anyone or anything other than Himself. Exodus 20 tells us that God is a jealous God and, as stated in the first five verses, does not want us bowing down (giving control) to anything except Himself. When we allow anything else to direct or control us, we violate one of the principal commandments; in fact the commandment we are told was the greatest commandment, "Thou shalt love the Lord thy God with all thy heart, and with all thy soul, and with all thy mind, and with all thy strength: this is the first commandment." (Matt. 22:37) We can be thankful that God is indeed a jealous God and will seek to reveal areas of submission which are not pleasing to Him so that our total submission might be unto Him alone, our Lord and Savior.

Another way in which the Lord helps us is through the example in the seventh chapter of Joshua. God knew there was sin, but Joshua didn't. God then allowed Joshua to know that something was wrong. Joshua did the right thing; he sought the Lord. Often, we realize something is wrong with our walk with the Lord, but we don't know what. God's answer to Joshua gives us guidance in how to pray for our answer. God said there is sin in the camp. (Joshua 7:10) So many times, when we know something is wrong, or when our Ai comes and our world seems to fall apart, we point to the circumstance and say, "If only this were different." Or we may blame God for allowing events to transpire as they have. This type of reaction reveals even more clearly where the problem may be, sin in the camp. And the camp is our heart. To learn to pray, "Lord, show me what is wrong in me that makes me defeated in this situation," is a great and glorious truth revealed by the story of Ai. As we look at other saints of the Bible, such as Paul and Silas, we find that, regardless of the outward situation, they were in the victory when their hearts were right with the Lord. In Acts 16:25 we read how they were beaten and thrown into prison, "At midnight Paul and Silas prayed, and sang praises unto God." They could have indeed been defeated and said, "If only we were not in prison, or if they just hadn't beaten us, then our walk with the Lord would be okay." The lesson to learn is that we should not think that changing circumstances is necessarily the answer, but rather when something is defeating us, we should pray, "Lord, show me what I need to learn in this situation." We may wish that God would change the people or circumstances around us, but if we get our hearts in the right place, we can be experiencing the peace and power of God in the midst of anything.

The scripture warns us to beware of the deceitfulness of sin, "lest any of you be hardened through the deceitfulness of sin." (Hebrews 3:13) Where there is sin, the enemy has his foot in the door. It is the devil himself who causes us to blame God for what we think is wrong. He uses our ignorance and lack of understanding to turn us away from the Lord. It is Satan himself who points to the circumstance to discourage us. Sin is truly deceitful, causing us to look everywhere else but within to find the problem. We do well to keep pressing on toward God and praying, "Lord, shine your light on the sin in my heart," so that we don't become hardened against God in our ignorance. If you feel like giving up, *don't*. Satan is the only one who desires that. In times of inner struggle, such as when Joshua was so badly discouraged after the defeat at Ai, we must never lose sight of the fact that because God is faithful, He will help us if we continue to humbly seek Him.

Philippians 4: 7 states, "And the peace of God, which passeth all understanding, shall keep your hearts and minds through Christ Jesus." When our hearts are free from sin, the peace of God keeps us regardless of our understanding of the things around us. Our understanding may tell us that the circumstance is dreadful, yet the peace of God keeps us through Christ Jesus. When our understanding of the circumstances causes us to be defeated, and we are not kept by the peace of God, it is an indication that something is wrong within. Our trials and testing can only defeat us when there is sin in our hearts. Circumstances have no power over the believer when God is properly and fully upon the throne of the heart.

A closing thought: The searchlight of the heart is God's. If we are humble before him, He is the one that reveals sin. Self-examination didn't reveal that Achan had sinned, God's Spirit did. We are not to be the seekers of sin, but the seekers and worshippers of God.

Who Hath Enabled Me

1 Timothy 1:12

Heavenly Father, how precious and wonderful is Your love toward us. Such a privilege it is to search out Your truths and to be taught by the Holy Spirit. Such a friend and comforter we have in Him who was sent to be with us until Jesus's glorious return. You are a sacred and holy God, may we approach you as such, and may our lives not bring reproach upon You in any way. For You have granted that we should bear Your name. Lord, let us not fail to seek to please You, and You alone. May we more identify with being crucified with Christ that You may live through us less hindered by self. In Jesus's name we pray. Amen.

How well Paul knew of what he spoke! Being enabled (empowered) for God's work by Jesus, Paul thought it quite amazing that from a background of utter defiance and hatred for the followers of Jesus he now was in the Lord's service. Paul gratefully says, "I thank Christ Jesus our Lord, who hath enabled me, for that he counted me faithful, putting me into the ministry, who was before a blasphemer, and a persecutor, and injurious." (1 Tim. 1:12) Even though miracles were wrought through the hands of Paul, yet he considered himself "chief among sinners" (1 Tim. 1:15). In Paul's words we can feel the deep emotion, appreciation, and humility as he says, "enabled ME... counted ME faithful... putting ME into the ministry." (1 Tim. 1:12)

Me of all people; me who consented to the death of Stephen (Acts 8: l); me who persecuted the church (Acts 8:1-3; 9:1-2); me who thought that I was walking pleasing before God after the manner of the fathers (Phil. 3:4-6; Acts 22:3-4); me of all men he enabled, counted faithful and put into the ministry!

In 1 Cor. 15:9 when Paul states, "For I am the least of the apostles, that am not meet to be called an apostle, because I persecuted the church of God," he was not making a false statement of humility. Paul, from the bottom of his heart, felt it was an amazing act of God's grace to allow him to be in the ministry after so violently persecuting the Lord's people. He meant it when he said he was the least. He meant it when he said he wasn't fit for the privileged calling. And indeed, for any sinner to be saved by the grace of God, it is equally a privileged calling. To think that we, who were in our sinful nature, disobedient to God and dead in our sins, should have the very special privilege of being forgiven of our sins and promised eternal life in the Kingdom of God, is certainly worthy of our deepest, heart felt gratitude!

There is a sacred beauty to the discovery Paul made that caused him to say "Christ Jesus... enabled me." (1 Tim 1:12) Before Paul saw this beauty and learned of the enabling of the Holy Spirit, he first saw how useless his own talents and credentials were of themselves. On his way to Damascus, Paul was confident in his Jewish heritage, his following of the Pharisees' beliefs, the teaching of Gamaliel (who was held in great respect among the people, under whom Paul had studied... Acts 5:34 & 22:3), and confident in his following of the law (Phil.3:4-6). In an instant, this confidence perished as Paul came face to face with Jesus and the power of the Holy Spirit (Acts 9). Paul clearly learned the difference between reliance upon self and reliance upon the person of the Holy Spirit. From that moment, Paul craved to know only Jesus and His power, and to trust in Him.

Paul paid a tremendous price of sacrifice to learn of the ways of the Spirit. In Paul's own words he says, was crucified with Christ and that he died daily. He saw so precisely that only through the Holy Spirit could he be effective in ministry that he actually cherished the loss of all things and welcomed the sacrifices, for they brought him closer to Jesus and into a greater understanding of the ways of the Holy Spirit. For we read in Phil. 3:7, "What things were gain to me, those I counted loss for Christ. Yea doubtless, and I count all things but loss for the excellency of the knowledge of Christ Jesus my Lord: for whom I have suffered the loss of all things, and do count them but dung, that I may win Christ."

So real to Paul were the things of the Spirit that in spite of all he suffered, from beatings, prison, and persecutions, he thanked Christ Jesus for putting him into the ministry. He did this without hesitation (Yea doubtless). (Phil 3:7) Paul had discovered something so precious, so sacred and so very special that all of life's experiences and riches could not for one moment entice him, for he had found Jesus and He was very real to Paul.

The enabling of God is a glorious and wonderful thing. It is likened unto a treasure chest full of every tool and every piece of equipment necessary for the job at hand. And the provisions of the Holy Spirit (through His enabling) are perfectly fitted to the task; absolutely perfectly fitted. But these tools are not accessible to man in the flesh. They are opened only unto the Holy Spirit. And the Holy Spirit utilizes vessels, enabling them with these very special and perfectly fitted tools. Vessels who have "suffered the loss of all things." (Phil. 3:8) Those who have been crucified with Christ! What are these tools? The gifts of the Holy Spirit. The power of the Holy Spirit! The wisdom and knowledge of the Holy Spirit! The love and compassion of the Holy Spirit! Paul knew about them, and they were so precious to him that everything else was but dung.

When someone has been enabled by the Holy Spirit for the work of God, that one will always speak reverently about the Father, the Son and the Holy Spirit. That one will always give God the glory and will stand with Paul in saying from the bottom of the heart, "I am not worthy to be called by His glorious name...for I am but a sinner saved by His grace." When people are enabled by the Holy Spirit, they see God as He is: holy, sacred, full of glory and compassion, and their work will reflect this great reverence for the things of God.

Blessed Jesus, bring us to the place of understanding
how precious Your enabling is, how holy is Your calling
and how sacred is the work of the Holy Spirit. May we
learn not to grieve Him and to better follow Him each
moment of our lives. In Jesus's name we pray. Amen.

Through The Eyes Of A Prophet

II Kings 6: 17

Heavenly Father, we are grateful for the Holy Spirit who abides with us daily through this life. We thank You for His teaching, for His guidance and help in every situation. We thank You for the strength and encouragement of Your word, which feeds our spirits and girds us with hope regardless of the circumstance. We thank you for the sacrifice of Jesus on the cross, for the shedding of His blood which cleanses our sins and grants us access into Your most holy presence. Let us learn to show You the reverence and respect due Your name. Teach us these things as we enter the inner sanctuary of worship and behold You in Your glory and majesty. In Jesus's name we pray. Amen

Elisha was a mighty prophet of God. In reading glimpses of his life, we are enlightened into seeing in the realm of the Spirit. This realm of faith looks beyond the appearance of things in this world and beholds God. Through the life of the prophet, God is beheld by the prophet and revealed unto many. Only what is beheld is revealed, for we can only share with others that which we ourselves have experienced and learned firsthand from God. This is the type of sharing which results in the manifestation of God, to the degree that we have experienced Him.

In 2 Kings 4 a poor widow is helped because of a miracle. With one pot of o the type of sharing those results in the manifestation of God, to the degree il, many empty vessels were filled to supply her need. This was not possible in the natural. The oil in the one container would have filled only a similar vessel, but in this case the oil kept flowing until many more were filled. Elisha gave these instructions because he was seeing in the realm of God; the realm that truly is the final authority in all things. Elisha had traveled with Elijah and had beheld the power of God through him. Perhaps this helped Elisha to know that such things were possible. As we read of His power in the Bible and claim the word as absolute truth, we gain a foundation for faith. The more we behold His power in the word, God causes our faith to rise.

To the one who sees as the prophet does, in the realm of God, what appears in the natural is not the final authority. The laws of nature, science and the physical realm are subject to the power of God. By the person of the Holy Spirit, God affects and changes things in the natural realm. Such acts of God give us a glimpse of the kingdom which is soon to come. We do not now see all, but partially. Even those mightily used of God such as Elisha and Paul proclaimed that they knew only in part. None of us knows everything. In 2 Kings 4:27 Elisha says, "the Lord hath hid it from me, and hath not told me." Paul states in 1 Corinthians 13:12, "now we see through a glass, darkly; but then face to face: now I know in part; but then shall I know even as also I am known." We know only that which we are given to know. It is nothing to boast about, for knowledge of the things of God is a gift from the revelations of the Holy Spirit. We have done nothing to obtain understanding, it is given to us by God. Not given to glorify the one receiving, but to glorify God. (1 Cor.4:7)

All that we learn is given to be used by the Holy Spirit for God's glory, not for the glory of the one used. In 2 Kings 5 we read the story of the healing of a leper named Naaman, who was a mighty captain of the host of Syria. As the story unfolds, this great captain comes to Elisha expecting him to perform some great deed or dramatic approach to healing. Elisha doesn't even come out of his house, but sends word of what Naaman is to do. Following the final compliance by Naaman, he is healed and returns to see Elisha. His words at that time were not praise for Elisha, but for God. "Now I know that there is no God in all the earth, but in Israel." (2 Kings 5:15) Here we see God, through the power of the Spirit, glorify Himself. The prophet was merely being an obedient vessel. Elisha could have used the revelation for his own glory and gain, but he refused. Such is the way God wishes us to use that which He gives.

Through Elisha we see God's healing power; we see the dead raised as told in 2 Kings 4; we see an entire army in pursuit of Elisha single-handedly led captive by him in chapter 6, and the power awaiting in the realm of the spirit is revealed to us as an army of chariots of fire are shown to Elisha (2 Kings 6: 17). This same power is here today. It is through faith awakened, and yielding the life completely to Him, that we begin to see glimpses of such things. Faith opens our eyes into the realm of all things being possible. Such understanding and faith are not given for us to control, but rather are given to provide God the opportunity to manifest and glorify Himself. We are not to use the things of the Spirit, but rather are to be used by the Spirit. There is a great difference. Elisha shows us how to be used by the Spirit, and refuse to use the things of the Spirit incorrectly.

Elisha saw, believed, and acted. Many beheld the results, but few pursued such a deeper relationship. Even among the prophets and their families we see in II Kings 6 that when the axe head fell into the river, it wasn't one of the sons of the prophets that believed to retrieve it, but Elisha. Somehow, he was connected enough in the realm of the Spirit to not let the natural laws limit his faith in God. Many may believe in God, but fewer are connected enough to act on their faith. Jesus encourages us to become those who act. In John

14:12 we read, "He that believeth on me, the works that I do shall he do also; and greater works than these shall he do."

The door is open to anyone who wishes to pay the price to follow Jesus. The more submission, the more sacrifice, the more death to self-will, the more one is prepared to be used of the Holy Spirit. Knowledge and belief without the foregoing leads more toward using the things of God, not being used of God.

Faith says, "I accept nothing in the natural as final or limiting; not cancer... not brain damage... not unbelief in one for whom we pray... not famine... not death... not an army of the enemy at the gates... not poverty." Elisha was not limited by any of these, and neither should we be. Faith says, "It may be there in the natural but I'm looking up... I see something beyond and something greater." Faith says, "I will pray…I will believe…I will trust in and wait upon the Lord." The greater clarity we have in understanding our own absolute helplessness, the better position we are in to see faith rise and God be manifest.

God's work in the heart makes us know that we can do nothing of His work...that we can offer not one good thing of ourselves... not one word... not one prayer... not one song that will bless unless He fills them with His Holy Spirit. In the realization of our helplessness faith rises to say, with God all things are possible. In 2 Kings 6-7 we read the dreadful story of a war and famine so bad that women were killing their own children for food. Through the word of the Lord, Elisha proclaimed that in one day the situation would totally turn into that of plenty. How could he say such a thing? In the natural it was impossible. He could say it because he knew in Whom he had believed and saw in the realm of the Spirit. God can do the same for us. Regardless of what challenges we may face in our lives, may God bring us into prayer and the deeper sanctuaries of worship until we begin to see Him, and all things, through the eyes of the prophet, the eyes of the Holy Spirit.

Because Thou Hast Put Thy Trust in Me

Jeremiah 39:18

Heavenly Father, we come to You seeking the peace which abides in Your presence. We find that our own minds become an enemy of peace and a source of worry and concern whenever our hearts are invaded with unbelief, or our eyes are departed from You. Whatever may touch our lives, it is certainly known by You, and we seek help in remembering to bring our concerns to You, particularly in letting them remain at Your feet. Too often, we churn over adversity (or the possibility thereof) in our minds to our own distraction from You, and find torment rather than peace. The common concerns of life have a way of consuming our thoughts. Surely, this is why You have said to cast all of our cares upon You. Teach us this discipline fully, that nothing may rob us of our abiding in Your peace. It is aptly writ ten that nothing shall separate us from the love of God. Bring this confidence into a daily reality and a fortress against any intruder, for nothing can enter to disturb our place in You unless we, through our own choosing, allow the gates to be opened. We seek Your strength and help in learning to keep the gates barred to any except You. In Jesus's name we pray. Amen.

In the commonplace of daily life, we may wonder how our lives stack up in the sight of God. Our efforts and accomplishments may seem dim by comparison to others. We may ask, "Does God take notice of my life?" or "Have I contributed anything to pleasing Him?" Jesus gave a heartening example of how much God takes notice, particularly of the little things which may go unnoticed by others. In Matt. 10:42 we read of Jesus saying, "whosoever shall give to drink unto one of these little ones a cup of cold water only in the name of a disciple, verily I say unto you, he shall in no wise lose his reward." God does indeed take notice of even the smallest things and counts them worthy of reward. From the widow's mite to a cup of cold water, God looks upon the heart to reward that which pleases Him with quantity having little importance.

There are two other examples of God's thoughts on similar matters in the book of Jeremiah. The 35th chapter is the story of a family, the Rechabites, whom God had noticed. In a time of rebellion against Him, and of disobedience to God's word, the Lord cites this family as an example of obedience to their father. Jeremiah is told to bring the family to the house of the Lord and put wine before them to drink. Jeremiah does so, but they refuse to drink saying, "we will drink no wine: for Jonadab the son of Rechab our father commanded us saying, Ye shall drink no wine, neither ye, nor your sons forever." (Jeremiah 35:6) The Lord then speaks to Jeremiah in verse 35:14 saying, "The words of Jonadab the son of Rechab that he commanded his sons not to drink wine, are performed; for unto this day they drink none, but obey their father's commandment: notwithstanding I have spoken unto you, rising early and speaking; but ye hearkened not unto me." Later in verse 18 and 19, we see how God blessed and honored this family for obeying their father's command. God had taken notice of this seemingly small matter. To God, this family was worthy of reward and notice as well as being used as an example to the entire nation of Israel. We read, "because ye have obeyed the commandment of Jonadab your father, and kept all his precepts, and done according unto all that he hath commanded you: Therefore, thus saith the Lord of hosts, the God of Israel; Jonadab the son of Rechab shall not want a man to stand before me forever." (Jeremiah 35:19)

Another story of similar events takes place in Jeremiah chapters 38 and 39. Ebedmelech, an Ethiopian eunuch in the house of King Zedekiah, takes it upon himself to help the prophet Jeremiah when all others were seeking to kill him. When Jeremiah is put in the dungeon to die, Ebedmelech seeks the King and requests that Jeremiah be set free. Ebedmelech was taking a very unpopular position in supporting Jeremiah, but he demonstrated the strength and trust in God which enabled him to take the proper stand. When princes in the kingdom were calling for Jeremiah's death, Ebedmelech stood to request his life. As we read in Jer. 38:9, "My lord the king, these men have done evil in all that they have done to Jeremiah the prophet, whom they have cast into the dungeon; and he is like to die for hunger in the place where he is." The king then allows Ebedmelech to take Jeremiah out of the dungeon. At this time, Jerusalem is under siege by Nebuchadnezzar, king of Babylon. The city is to be destroyed and the people taken captive. In the middle of this war and destruction, God speaks to Jeremiah to go to Ebedmelech and tell him, "Thus saith the Lord of hosts, the God of Israel; behold I will bring my words upon this city for evil, and not for good; and they shall be accomplished in that day before thee. But I will surely deliver thee, and thou shalt not fall by the sword, but thy life shall be for a prey unto thee: because thou hast put thy trust in me, saith the Lord." (Jer. 39:16-18)

How encouraging to note that indeed God does see the little things that go on behind the scenes and rewards accordingly. He rewards consistent obedience to Him in the common places of our lives just as surely as He noticed the actions of Jonadab and Ebedmelech.

Lift Up Now Thine Eyes

Genesis 13:14

Heavenly Father, Your ways are often not clear to us for our eyes are not always keen in the Spirit. For what we lack in understanding, please grant us an extra measure of faith and trust in You. Forgive us for the errors of our ignorance and grant unto us a clearer knowledge of Yourself. Accept as evidence of our sincerity the fact that we come to You. We come to You in the reading of Your word, and we come to You in prayer and worship. We come for there is no one else for us to approach. There are no answers outside of You. We come and offer ourselves before Your throne wanting to know You more fully. We thank You for Your patience and love and for the shed blood of Jesus, which is the ever-perfect cleansing for our sins. Beneath the blood we stand, for it has purchased us the boldness to approach Your most holy throne. Wash us afresh, and continue to draw us into the fullness of Your purpose in Christ Jesus our Lord. In Jesus's name we pray. Amen.

In Genesis 12 we begin to read of God's calling upon Abraham to separate himself, for God would make of his seed a great nation. Abraham then goes forth in faith not fully understanding all that would unfold before him. In verse 7, God appears to Abraham and promises that He will give to Abraham's seed this land in which Abraham is wandering. The next thing we see is that there is a famine in the land. After following God's direction and worshipfully building altars along the way, and listening to God's words of promise, Abraham finds himself in a famine. He then *moves* onward into Egypt for he could no longer stay in the land; the famine was so grievous. Often along the path of following Jesus, we may find ourselves in a situation likened unto the famine Abraham found. We may have obeyed and in faith followed, only to find something other than what we had in mind. *Never* should we doubt our Lord, for He sees in an eternal perspective. The experiences we go through are necessary for God to accomplish what He wishes in our hearts.

As we read on, we find that during the famine, while in Egypt, God caused Abraham to be treated very well. "And he entreated Abram well... and he had sheep, and oxen, and he asses, and menservants, and maidservants and she asses and camels." (Genesis 12:16) When Abraham left Egypt, we read in Genesis 13:2, "And Abram was very rich in cattle, in silver, and in gold." We can take encouragement from this event, for it is assured that we will come forth from every famine situation with spiritual riches of greater faith, greater trust in God, and a closer relationship with Him as we keep our eyes upon Him in each situation. The place we find ourselves may seem desolate, but as we seek the Lord in His word, He will reveal more of Himself to us, bringing forth springs of living water in the midst of desolation.

We see that God had so blessed Abraham and his nephew Lot, that the land was not large enough to hold both of them. As we see in Genesis 13:6-7, "And the land was not able to bear them, that they might dwell together: for their substance was great, so that they could not dwell together. And there was strife between the herdsmen of Abram's cattle and the herdsmen of

Lot's cattle." At this point we are shown a wonderful lesson in the heart and mind of God, as well as insight to the heart of Abraham. Abraham approaches Lot, his nephew, and says, "Let there be no strife I pray thee, between me and thee, and between my herdsmen and thy herdsmen; for we be brethren. Is not the whole land before thee? Separate thyself, I pray thee, from me: if thou wilt take the left hand, then I will go to the right; or if thou depart to the right hand, then I will go to the left." (Genesis 13:8) Abraham, the elder as well as Lot's uncle, was giving his nephew the choice of the land. Here we see the man to whom God had made the promise of the entire area, being totally open and releasing control into the hands of God. Abraham thought, "Take what you will Lot, I will take what God leaves me." Abraham did not say, "God has promised this to me, so I will take the best for myself." This is an admirable quality in the heart of Abraham. (Lord grant that we might seek such a heart attitude, and see what God would do for us.)

We then read of Lot lifting his eyes and looking over the land. He notices that the plain of Jordon, over toward Sodom and Gomorrah, is well watered "even as the garden of the Lord." (Genesis 13:10) So, he chooses what looks the best to his natural eye. His spiritual eyes were closed, for we go on to read of how wicked the cities of Sodom and Gomorrah were. We find later in Genesis that Lot loses everything during the destruction of Sodom and Gomorrah, where he eventually lived. Often the best appearing choice is not the best choice for us spiritually. On the other hand, even famine, poverty and adversity may yield the greatest of blessings to the one whose heart is right with the Lord. In Genesis 13: 14-17 we read the beautiful response of God to Abraham after Lot had made his choice saying, "Lift up now thine eyes, and look from the place where thou art northward, and southward, and eastward, and westward: for all the land which thou seest, to thee will I give it, and to thy seed forever. And I will make thy seed as the dust of the earth." God had watched as

Abraham allowed Lot to lift his eyes and choose. Then God turns to Abraham and says, "lift up now thine eyes." (Genesis 13:14) The Lord rejoices to bless those whom He has chosen and those whose hearts are right before Him. We are better off to let God direct our path than to use our own human opinion outside of Him as Lot did. Though one may choose this world's best, it cannot compare to the spiritual joys of walking with Jesus. Praise God!

Today's Righteousness, Tomorrow's Reward

Gal. 6:9

Heavenly Father, Your ways are past finding out. Through all things You guide and direct for our good, though we may not understand the sequence of events. Truly You come to the aid of those who put their faith in You though we be laden with infirmities and imperfections. How marvelous it is to consider Your keen interest in our lives, an interest we have done nothing to generate and can do little to maintain. It is Your nature to be concerned and loving toward Your creation. We are the recipients of great grace from You, and as we realize the magnitude of Your love and effort on our behalf, we bow before You and express our gratefulness. Thank You Lord. You have done more for us than we could ask or think. In Jesus's name we pray. Amen.

The book of Esther is a marvelous picture of God using a person to accomplish His purpose while blessing that one for obedience. We see God using those who did not believe and piecing together events of the past to direct future events. There are many high points to the story upon which we will focus.

The scene was the kingdom of Ahasuerus into which the Jews had previously been carried away as captives. Through a series of events, the king decided to take a new queen, and a search was made of all the fair women of the land. Esther, Mordecai's niece, was one of the young women considered. Mordecai and Esther were Jews living in this foreign land, and we watch as God was yet very involved in their lives as events unfolded. A New Testament passage which relates this concept is 1 Cor. 7:18-24. It concludes by saying, "Let every man, wherein he is called therein abide with God." (1 Cor 7:24) As out of place as we may feel in this world, it is encouraging to see God's interest and involvement in the lives of His people who indeed were in a foreign land and out of place.

Esther was finally chosen to be queen, and the king now had a Jewish queen, although she had been instructed of Mordecai to not reveal this to anyone. While this was going on, Mordecai overheard a plot to kill the king. He faithfully reported the matter, and the plot was uncovered and prevented. A record of the event was written mentioning Mordecai as the person who revealed the evil plot. It is interesting to note that we see a captive Jew working for the good of his captor king. We see God opening doors in the earthly kingdom of Ahasuerus for His children, to later be beneficial to His people. Mordecai and Esther were living their lives, mindful of God yet unable to see the master plan at the time each step was taken.

After this event, the king promoted an evil-hearted man named Haman. Everyone bowed before Haman except Mordecai. This greatly angered Haman and he sought the king's permission to destroy, not Mordecai alone, but all of the Jews in all of the land. The king granted his request. When everything looked good with Esther as queen, a tremendous testing had come to Mordecai and Esther. God had not left them, nor had He placed them where they would be humiliated or ruined as it appeared. He had placed them where they were, for a specific reason soon to be revealed. Mordecai then sent word to Esther to petition the king for her people, saying, "For if thou altogether holdest thy peace at this time, then shall there enlargement and deliverance arise to the Jews from another place... and who knoweth whether thou art come to the kingdom for such a time as this?" (Esther 4:14) The events had unfolded, the people were in position, and yet Mordecai with faith believed that even if Esther were too fearful to speak, deliverance would yet arise to the Jews. Esther then asked for prayer and fasting of the people for three days before she made her request to the king. Ester acknowledged, "So will I go in unto the king, which is not according to the law: and if I perish, I perish." (Esther 4:16) There is no guarantee that those in the right place at the right time will fulfill God's plan, but what a tragedy if they miss the opportunity to participate in what He is doing!

Esther then prepared to request deliverance for her people, but prior to the final day when she was to ask, God moved to prepare the way for her. This is a strong indication that the prayers and fasting of the people were certainly being heard and acted upon. The night before her request of the king, the king could not sleep and asked to have the records of the kingdom read to him. During the reading, the story of Mordecai uncovering the plot to kill the king was read. The king decided to honor Mordecai, the man whom Haman was anxious to kill. Of all the records which could have been read, God caused this record of Mordecai to come before the king. How beautiful to see how righteous acts quietly build for godly results in the future. So it is with much of our daily labor. How marvelous it is to behold God working behind the scenes. He answers the prayers of His people while they yet can see nothing. The king was sleepless and requested the records. Because of Mordecai's past proper actions, we see God using this in a great way. We should never lose heart in well doing as we read in Gal. 6:9, "and let us not be weary in well doing: for in due season, we shall reap if we faint not." Mordecai could have justified an attitude of "why should I help the king who holds us as captive" and not done the proper thing. How much better that he did do right regardless of his circumstances. In this story, God's words of we shall reap are profound, for not only does Mordecai benefit, but all of the Jews in the kingdom as well. (Gal.

6:9) This is certainly a clear incentive to keep a proper heart attitude in all that we would do.

In the balance of the story, we see rapid answer to prayer with Haman being destroyed, the Jews delivered and Mordecai advanced in the kingdom to the benefit of all the Jews. The story is brimming with truth for our lives today. Today's righteous acts will set the foundation for future fulfillment of God's purposes. God does hear and answer prayer, moving often invisibly to the petitioner yet never deaf to His children's cries. God holds all people and nations in His hands and directs the course of events in mysterious ways. Those who step forward in His name in the time and power of His Spirit will surely be blessed.

Who Art Thou, Lord?

Acts 9:5

Heavenly Father, we come to You having yet so much to learn
and having only begun to grow in Your grace. Our understanding
is not perfect and our sins and errors You see far more clearly
than we do. Thank You for Your great patience with us and for
Your faithfulness towards us always despite our imperfection.
We thank You for the faith to stand upon Your word. A faith
which You honor, not because of our good works, but because
we believe in Your great work upon the cross. With that as our
foundation, we come boldly to seek Your touch for all who suffer
and are in need. Pour Your Spirit out upon the lost, the sick
and the bound. Grant that our requests which we bring to You
would be fulfilled to the glory of the name in which we pray...
Jesus. Thank you for answering prayer, in Jesus's name. Amen.

The story of Paul's conversion is rich with spiritual lessons that are
helpful to each of us in our walk with Jesus. As we ponder the life of
Paul, we learn that he took God seriously and endeavored to do that
which he thought was correct. In Acts 22:3 we read, "I am verily a
man which am a Jew, born in Tarsus, a city in Cilicia, yet brought
up in this city at the feet of Gamaliel, and taught according to the
perfect manner of the law of the fathers, and was zealous toward
God, as ye all are this day." Paul had knowledge about God prior

to knowing God, and yet for all of his knowledge his response to Jesus in Acts 9:5 was, "who art thou, Lord?" Paul didn't know the person of God about whom he had received knowledge. The question then is, how can we learn to know the person of God through the knowledge we are able to glean from His word?

Part of the answer is to understand the purpose of knowledge. Why do we read and study? Why do we listen to teaching about God? If our answer is to gain knowledge only, then we miss the purpose of God in giving us knowledge. Paul says very clearly in Philippians 3:10 that the purpose of learning is, "that I may know Him and the power of His resurrection, and the fellowship of His sufferings, being made conformable unto His death." To know Him is one of the purposes of gaining knowledge. A second desired result of learning is stated in Ephesians 4:13, "Till we all come in the unity of the faith, and of the knowledge of the Son of God, unto a perfect man, unto the measure of the stature of the fullness of Christ." To be transformed into His likeness is then a second purpose of learning.

Before either one of these two desired results can become a reality to some degree in our lives, the yielding of our wills from the heart must accompany knowledge. Knowledge, without yielding and the proper heart attitude, produces only inflated religious egos and self-righteousness. Paul said, after listing all of the qualifications he had as a Jew, "Yea doubtless, and I count all things but loss for the excellency of the knowledge of Christ Jesus my Lord: for whom I have suffered the loss of all things, and do count them but dung, that I may win Christ, and be found in him, not having mine own righteousness, which is of the law." (Phil. 3:8-9)

Paul had knowledge, and then he met Jesus. The next thing that happened was an inner yielding of the heart which allowed God to illuminate the knowledge Paul had received. We read in Acts 9:6, "And he (Paul) trembling and astonished said, Lord, what wilt thou have me to do." From that moment Paul was heading down the right path. Submission was joined with knowledge and the results were very clear when we see how God used Paul.

Knowledge of God could be likened to the coffee grinds waiting for the water to be poured over them to produce the coffee. Yielding the heart to God causes Him to pour His Spirit over the things we learn, and the results are rivers of living water flowing out of the believer's innermost being. Without yielding we have only the letter of the word. Yielding produces the living Spirit of the word manifest in the life of the believer. We can hear the word and see and read it, but if we don't yield to Him, it will profit us very little. We read in Acts 28 that it takes hearing, seeing, as well as understanding with the heart, before our lives are converted into something pleasing to God; "lest they should see with their eyes, and hear with their ears, and understand with their heart, and should be converted, and I should heal them." (Acts 28:27) It is possible to hear and see without yielding the heart, but it is impossible to be converted without yielding the heart. A transformed life is only possible when we yield the will to God.

Knowing Him will sustain us when our understanding may fail us. We may not understand why a loved one must suffer, but knowing Jesus will put us where He will carry us through. We may not understand why it appears that God doesn't answer our prayers, but knowing Him will comfort our hearts in the times of waiting. We may not understand how the power of God is manifest, but knowing Him will give us the boldness to call upon His name for healing and deliverance, and will loosen our faith to believe God for the needs of another to be met. We may not know why adversity strikes when undeserved, but knowing Him gives us the strength to yet praise Him regardless of what we may face. When we are tried and tested, may God grant us the grace to not forget that part of the process of knowing Him is as Paul said, "that I may know... the fellowship of His sufferings, being made conformable to His death." (Phil. 3:10) Surely this is part of the inner work of the cross that makes more room for Him within us.

If we do not make room for Him in our hearts by yielding self-will to Him, then the life-giving power of knowledge and the transforming power of knowledge is not unlocked. Colossians 2:3 tells us that all of the treasures of wisdom and knowledge are hidden in God, therefore, it is God we must make room for in our hearts before the treasures begin to be unlocked. There are no shortcuts to gaining the living knowledge of our Lord. Spiritual understanding comes to us a little bit at a time as we surrender a little more of ourselves to Jesus.

And There Came a Lion, And A Bear

1 Sam. 17:34

Heavenly Father, many are the challenges that daily face Your children. At times our hearts are overwhelmed by the appearance of what has come against us. Oh Lord, help us to keep our eyes upon You, alone, for we desperately need Your strength and comfort. Let us not be deceived by the appearance of any situation, for You are greater than any enemy that would assail us. Help us to learn from each day and each challenge that Your unfailing love and abiding presence are forever near, as You have promised. Particularly comfort those whose hearts are breaking due to the multitude of distresses that have touched their lives. Pour out of Your Spirit upon all who earnestly seek You, and in the midst of trouble reveal Yourself to the hearts of those who so need to see. Praise You and thank You for Your comfort and love. In Jesus's name we pray. Amen.

It is certainly a part of God's plan that we be tested and tried as He works to develop us into the image of His Son. The scripture refers to fiery trials, which denotes something more than a minor experience. Yet we do not always look upon our challenges in the light of scripture, particularly in the heat of the turmoil. Much can be learned from the story of David in 1 Samuel 17 concerning the victorious life we are promised in Christ. We must remember that God never allows anything to destroy us, but rather desires us to rise in victory above each and every adversity. Even as David said, "Many are the afflictions of the righteous: but the Lord delivereth him out of them all." (Psalm 34: 19)

As David kept his father's sheep, a lion came and sought to kill one of the lambs. Also, a bear had come and attempted the same. These were no little challenges when given the setting: alone in the fields with no protection, and predatory animals seeking to kill. David's response to the challenge was courageous. He did not avoid the challenge but rather went after the lion and the bear. He did not fear that which had come to destroy. He faced it with determination and trust in God. We read, "And I went out after him, and smote him, and delivered it out of his mouth: and when he arose against me, I caught him by his beard, and smote him, and slew him. Thy servant slew both the lion and the bear." (1 Sam. 17:35-36)

Upon these past victories, David built courage to face a bigger challenge, one for which God had been preparing him... Goliath and the armies of the Philistines. David knew that God had helped him with the lion and the bear, and as he saw the enemy defying the army of Israel he boldly proclaimed, "the Lord that delivered me out of the paw of the lion, and out of the paw of the bear, he will deliver me out of the hand of this Philistine." (1 Sam. 17:37) Had there been no lion and no bear in David's past, there would have been no foundation for the greater challenge and purpose of God. At times we may question the lion and the bear in our lives as we face certain adversities and challenges, but thank God for Scriptural examples that give us understanding as to the ways of God. Regardless of the situation, God always has our best at heart and uses all things to do His work in our hearts. As we confidently hold this to be true, we can face any adversity or challenge with courage.

The appearance of the lion and the bear were life threatening. David did not ask for these challenges, but they touched his life.

He looked past the appearance and fearfulness of the situations to trust in God concerning his lion and bear experience. The next challenge which he faced looked much worse. Goliath was a giant of such great stature that not one of the warriors in the entire army of Israel would accept his challenge to battle. Behind Goliath stood the massive army of the Philistines. As David looked upon Goliath and the opposing army, he did not see an undefeatable foe, but rather saw God's ability to bring victory in the face of such odds. David's trust was not in his own skill or ability as a warrior. He even refused to wear the protective armor that Saul had offered him. He was not going to face Goliath defensively with protective armor, he was going to face him with the victory already sure because of his trust in the living God. David's armor was his faith in God.

As David went to meet Goliath, the giant proclaimed, "Come to me, and I will give thy flesh unto the fowls of the air, and to the beasts of the field." (1 Sam. 17:44) Often our challenges shout similar taunting words at our hearts: "this will destroy you" or "you can't get out of this situation" or "you are hopelessly defeated." David responded from a platform of trust and unshakable faith in God saying, "Thou comest to me with a sword, and with a spear, and with a shield: but I come to thee in the name of the Lord of hosts, the God of the armies of Israel, whom thou hast defied. This day will the Lord deliver thee into mine hand; and I will smite thee, and take thine head from thee; and I will give the carcasses of the host of the Philistines this day unto the fowls of the air, and to the wild beasts of the earth; that all the earth may know that there is a God in Israel. And all this assembly shall know that the Lord saveth not with sword and spear: for the battle is the Lord's and he will give you into our hands." (1 Sam. 17:45-47)

We may feel that we do not have the proper sword or spear to be victorious over the particular challenge we face, but praise God our victory is not based upon our abilities or skills but upon our faith in Jesus. From a platform of faith, we can face any adversity, sickness, disease, trial or challenge and proclaim: "You may have come to destroy me, and you may appear to have that ability, but I face you with courage in my faith in God. And in His name, you have no power to destroy me. My victory is assured in Him." We can embrace and engage any challenge knowing we shall be triumphant in our God, in His victory and power.

David ran forward to Goliath with a sling and a few small stones, and a great faith in God. God guided the stone into the giant's skull and the victory was David's. God will guide our faith to victory in our lives as we, like David, charge forward. Let us find encouragement from this example given us in scripture and use the power of faith to embrace our challenges with expectant victory in our Lord.

And The Peace of God Shall Keep Your Hearts and Minds

Phil. 4:7

Dearest Heavenly Father, there is so much we need to learn about walking in Your peace in step with Your Spirit. We are anxious about far too many things. We take into our own hands that which is to be left in Yours. Our vision is blurred by the rush of the world around us. Help us to find that place of quiet, in Your presence, that we might be refreshed and focused upon You alone.

May we learn that our answers come when we are still before You, having quieted our minds so that we might hear You. Keep us in Your peace that our thoughts and actions will be breathed upon by Your Spirit and not the turmoil of all that is outside of You. Praise You and thank You for Your instruction and comfort given us through the Holy Spirit. In Jesus's name we pray. Amen.

Scripture says that the Lord left us His peace. Many of the New Testament letters begin with a greeting inclusive of peace. The term stimulates visions of quiet pools and gentle streams that quiet the soul and refresh the spirit. Yet in this world, a place of peace seems forever elusive. Thoughts and fears and concerns pertaining to life's daily challenges seek to flood our minds and bring turmoil to the soul.

Keeping pace with the basic responsibilities of life seems to chip away at any comfort of peace we may have found in a quiet moment with God. We can feel very unprotected from the harshness of the world around us and vulnerable to forces we do not want to influence us. We want peace of mind and a quiet joyful heart. Yet the flood gates of torment and turmoil can seem to be opened upon us, we find ourselves swept up in anxiety and concern, and peace has once again escaped our grasp. What is the secret to this peace of which Jesus speaks?

"And the peace of God, which passeth all understanding shall keep your hearts and minds through Christ Jesus." (Phil. 4: 7) We are told here that God's peace will keep our hearts and minds. It is worthy to note that this includes both the heart and the mind. There is a connection! A heart at peace is impossible without a peaceful mind. The mind is the target for turmoil and torment born of the enemy to rob the child of God of His peace. If the mind entertains thoughts of fear and doubt sown from the enemy, then the heart is in turmoil as a result. Sometimes, it is as though we enter a whirlwind of doubt and uncertainty, and peace has fled. We can be assured that the evil one is attempting to move us from resting in God. We must exercise caution in the midst of such a storm, so that our actions and decisions are not prompted by outside forces contrary to the moving of God. When the dust of the storm subsides...in the quiet that follows... we shall know the voice of God and His peace. (It is no wonder that the scripture speaks of girding up the loins of our minds and of the need for a helmet. 1 Peter l:13; Ephesians 6:17)

One might ask, "If the peace of God is supposed to keep my heart and mind, why is it that He can't seem to keep mine?" The problem is not that He can't keep us in His peace, but rather that we keep allowing things to come between us and His peace. We must learn to reject those thoughts that are fiery darts of the wicked or whirlwinds of confusion from Satan, and seek the shelter of

God's peace. Philippians 4:6 reads, "Be careful for nothing; but in everything by prayer and supplication with thanksgiving let your requests be made known unto God." (Phil. 4:6) In other words, "Don't be worried or dwell upon the concerns that may touch your life, not even one of them. Talk your Lord about every one of them. Let thanksgiving fill your heart, for you know He hears you and cares about every detail of your life."

In His peace things become clear; problems shrink, and guidance and wisdom are *ever* present. Peace is an immensely powerful thing, for the one who dwells in God's peace becomes a vessel which can be used of the Spirit. It is no wonder that the evil one seeks to remove us from that place of peace in God, for our effectiveness in God's plan is greatly reduced when we cease to be kept by His peace.

When wrestling with the torment which robs of peace, praise and worship are sure to restore us to that quiet place in God. In worship there is no place for other thoughts. The powers of darkness are scattered by the light and power of God's presence.

The Consequences
of Sin

Jer. 29:10-11

Heavenly Father, we are easily confused and dismayed by certain
things which come into our lives. We do not always correctly
interpret the intentions of that which You allow. Help us to see
that You only have thoughts of good toward Your children. Never,
even when we go astray, do You desire anything but the best for
us. We may need to go through unpleasant and difficult times as
a result of our own error, or because You see it is necessary for our
growth, but even then, Your desires toward us are that of love and
goodness. As a father chastens his children, so You chasten and
correct those You love. Thank You for Your faithful involvement
in our lives. May we never allow circumstances to cause us to
question Your love for us. In Jesus's name we pray. Amen.

Certain actions (or failure to act) will result in a consequence of that
action. This is true in the natural realm of life and in the realm of
the Spirit. If we are caught stealing, then we are likely to experience
the consequence of some punishment. If we are found faithful and
ambitious in the world of employment, then we are likely to be
promoted or find success. In the realm of the Spirit, if we yield
and obey God's word, giving the Holy Spirit control of our life, we

are postured to experience God's blessing. If we sin against God (whether known to others or not), then we are likely to experience a consequence of such disobedience.

Scripture shows us many examples of the consequences of sin, and more importantly, how God looks upon us during the consequence experience. There is often a stigma attached to us during the consequence by other people. This is quite distant from God's feelings toward us. When King David committed adultery and planned the murder of the woman's husband (2 Sam. 11), God sent Nathan, the prophet, to confront David with his sin. David immediately confessed his sin and was informed that God had also put his sin away. (2 Sam. 12:13) God had forgiven David of adultery and murder. (Such an undeserved and complete forgiveness of these sins should not strike us as amazing. Jesus demonstrated this love of God toward us when He gave His life on the cross to redeem man from sin.) However, there were consequences from the sin that God did not remove! The child of the adulterous act died. David fled from the throne, from his own son, and suffered the grief of both these experiences. Important to note is the fact that once the sin was confessed and God had forgiven David, David remained in fellowship and communion with God *even during the consequences.* In 2 Sam. 12:15-20 we read that David fasted and prayed for the child. After the child's death, David worshiped. When he fled from his son Absalom, we read that upon reaching the top of the mountain on his way out of the city, David worshiped God and prayed (2 Sam. 15:31-32). Later in 2 Sam. 17 we see this prayer was answered. The beauty of this truth is that we do not lose fellowship with God because of what we may go through as a result of the consequence of sin or ignorance. We only lose fellowship with God through sin and rebellion which is not confessed by us and forgiven by God. While David suffered a great deal of grief in his own heart, and the abusive treatment of some who observed the consequences of his sin coming to pass (2 Sam. 16:5-8), he never lost fellowship with the Lord. He had confessed his sin and was truly sorry for his mistake.

In Jeremiah we read of the captivity of Israel under the hand of King Nebuchadnezzar, king of Babylon. During this time of bondage, Israel experienced the consequence of turning away from the Lord. The Lord said, that because of their rebellion and disobedience, they would experience seventy years of captivity. This was not pleasant. They were driven from their homes and their land into a foreign nation as captives. Yet in the midst of this experience, the Lord revealed His feelings toward them through Jeremiah. Jer. 29:10-11 says, "After seventy years be accomplished at Babylon I will visit you, and perform my good word toward you, in causing you to return to this place. For I know the thoughts that I think toward you, saith the Lord, *thoughts of peace, and not of evil,*to give you an expected end." God's thoughts and heart motives are always good toward His children, regardless of what experience we must endure on the pathway of learning His ways.

Following King David's rule, his son Solomon reigned over Israel. During his leadership, Solomon turned away from the Lord significantly. As a result, so did the people. As a consequence, for this sin, God took most of the kingdom from David's family and gave the leadership to another. (Splitting the kingdom into two.) In 1 Kings chapter 11 God chose Jeroboam as the ruler of Israel and promised to make his kingdom and leadership sure if Jeroboam walked in God's ways (verses 37-38). Once made king, Jeroboam did not find it in his heart to trust in God's good intentions for him and his kingdom. He became fearful that if the people still went to Jerusalem to God's temple to worship, they would return to King Rehoboam (David's descendant) who still ruled over that portion of the original kingdom. (1 Kings 12:27) Many terrible future consequences could have been avoided if only Jeroboam would have trusted in God's word and believed God's good intentions toward him and the people of Israel. Had he known God and trusted in Him he would have prayed, "Lord, You came to give me the kingdom. I did not ask for it. You decided to split Israel because of Solomon's sin as You told me. I will believe in Your protection and wisdom, Lord, and

I will encourage the people of my kingdom to still go to the house of the Lord in Jerusalem to worship. My future, and the future of Your people, is in Your hands. I believe that Your intentions toward me and Israel are good, even as You have said. Give me strength to do that which is right in Your sight, even as we go through the consequence experience brought upon us by Solomon's sin." Had Jeroboam found it in his heart to pray such a prayer, God certainly would have honored his promise to establish Jeroboam's kingdom. How sad to read that Jeroboam and all his descendants were cut off from the face of the earth because he failed to trust in God's love and protection in the middle of God carrying out the consequences of Solomon's sin. (1 Kings 14: 7-16)

God desires to maintain fellowship with each of us continually, even during the consequences we go through as a result of our error. Surely, all things that work together for good include the consequence experiences. (Rom. 8:28) However, we are wise to avoid sin in the first place, for by doing so we avoid the often-unpleasant experiences that result from sin.

Lord, help us to see that all of Your intentions and thoughts toward us are good and only good. In the course of life, as we experience many different things, keep us from ever doubting Your love. May we never judge or question Your love by the circumstances through which we must navigate. Those You love, You chasten, and Your expected end for us is greater fellowship with You, which is for eternity! May we always quickly seek forgiveness for sin and error, that we may not for a moment be cut off from fellowship with You. May we commit to worship in times of blessing, in times of testing, and in times of consequence experiences. In Jesus's name we pray. Amen.

The Full Circle of The Blessedness of Giving

Luke 6:38

Heavenly Father, we come to this place of prayer with hearts that are amazed at the depth of Your unconditional love. We stand awed and humbled as we realize that Your compassion and longsuffering cause Your care to reach past our unrighteousness, past our shortcomings and gives to us the comforts of Your love. Your gentle wooing and constant desire to forgive are powerful forces which draw our seeking, though imperfect, hearts to You. With each new glimpse of You, granted us by the enlightening of the word and the Holy Spirit, we recognize how vast and unsearchable is our God, and how much more we have yet to learn. We worship You! We thank You! We give ourselves to You afresh, for Your love has drawn us to You. Fulfill Your eternal purpose in our lives. In Jesus's name we pray. Amen.

Jesus taught that it was more blessed to give than to receive. Paul encouraged the Christian to remember this teaching saying, "I have shewed you all things, how that so laboring ye ought to support the weak, and to remember the words of the Lord Jesus, how he said, 'It is more blessed to give than to receive." (Acts 20:35) We are further prompted to give generously, by the words of the Lord in Luke 6:38,

"Give and it shall be given unto you; good measure, pressed down, and shaken together, and running over, shall men give into your bosom. For with the same measure that ye mete withal it shall be measured to you again." The promise of blessing is certainly clear. However, there are things which can get in the way of our receiving God's blessing because of our giving.

Giving has many avenues of expression. There is the giving of time to the work and will of the Lord. There is the giving of our substance, our money, and our possessions unto others as guided by the Spirit. There is the giving of prayer on behalf of a needy soul. There is the giving of our service to help our fellow man with acts of kindness and caring, from the offer of a bowl of hot soup to continued care for a suffering loved one. The key to the blessedness which is spoken of is in the heart of the giver. More specifically, it is the heart attitude of the giver.

What is my inner motive for giving? Why do I give my money, my time, my talent or my service? This is where my own imperfections can cause me to stumble and fall before I reach the blessedness promised. I do not desire to stumble, and I may not even see why my giving does not yield the fullness of joy in my heart. Often, patterns developed from childhood, and inner voids not yet filled with the character of Jesus prevent my entering the blessed flow of giving. I may give with the desire for recognition, acknowledgement, or approval from those to whom I give. This motive will rob me of God's blessing. The word teaches that giving is to be in secret. By this Jesus means that the mechanics of giving are a private matter between the giver and God, not the giver and the receiver. My attitude about giving should be to please Him, not to receive anything from the one to whom I may give. This is true whether I am giving service, prayer, or financial support. Jesus clearly explains that the only way the blessedness comes is when the attitude and heart motives are correct. In fact, if they are not, there is no way we can expect to receive His blessing. "Take heed that ye do not your alms before men, to be seen of them: otherwise ye have no reward of your Father which is in heaven. Therefore, when thou doest thine alms, do not sound a trumpet before thee, as the hypocrites do in the synagogues and in the streets, that they may have glory of men. Verily I say unto you, they have their reward. But when thou doest alms, let not thy left hand know what thy right hand doeth: that thine alms may be in secret: and thy Father which seeth in secret himself shall reward thee openly. And when thou prayest, thou shalt not be as the hypocrites are: for they love to pray standing in the synagogues and in the corners of the streets, that they may be seen of men. Verily I say unto you, they have their reward. But thou, when thou prayest, enter into thy closet and when thou hast shut thy door, pray to thy Father which is in secret; and thy Father which seeth in secret shall reward thee openly." (Matt. 6:1-6)

When I give with the wrong heart motive, or from flawed motives which I may not clearly see, bitterness and resentment may be the frequent results in my own heart. If I do not receive the recognition hoped for, or the response I inwardly need, I may eventually begin to resent the receiver of my giving. In fact, I believe that God will purposely prevent the desired response to weed out the improper attitude in my heart. There were many sacrifices of old that were never accepted by the Lord, because the hearts of the givers were far from Him. (See Isaiah 1: 11 and Isaiah 29: 13.) The glorious working of the Holy Spirit is in those secret areas of my heart where He continues to conform me into the image of Christ. This is why He must prevent me from experiencing the fullness of joy in giving if my motive or attitude is incorrect; not to keep me from blessing, but to remove my flaws so I may experience the fullness of His richest blessing.

Another pitfall in giving is the danger of building self-righteousness and pride. I am reminded of the story of the Pharisee which prayed boastfully before the Lord about his giving, tithing and fasting, only to find that he was not justified before God. His heart was not adjusted properly by the Holy Spirit. (See Luke 18:9-14.) This problem can be avoided by following the advice of the Lord to "not let the left hand know what the right hand doeth." (Matt. 6:3) We are not to think upon our giving as though we were to receive a gold star or increased reward for each action. Let God keep the records, and let us keep on giving with abandon to the glory of Him Whom we serve.

The blessedness and joy of giving spoken about by the Lord must come full circle from His hand, or they will not come at all. We should never look to the receiver as the one who must be the giver of our reward for giving. God may or may not intend to bless in this way. We will find the richest of blessings when we are satisfied to receive from the hand of God our rewards for the privilege of giving. Paul articulated this attitude by saying, "I will very gladly spend and be spent for you; though the more abundantly I love you, the less I be loved." (2 Cor. 12: 15) Not only is this proper motive giving a blessing to the giver, it is also much more likely to bless the ones who receive and cause them to desire and draw near to God. Giving from the wrong motive platform tends to alienate the receiver, or even worse, may cause a relationship of bondage which is built out of obligation instead of love. If a person feels obligated to feed back to us the adulation, approval, or loyalty we improperly seek, our giving has a damaging effect. Proper giving should result primarily in thankfulness to God. (See 2 Cor. 9: 11-13) Holy Spirit-led giving has no strings attached. The blessings flow full circle back to us from the Lord and are in no way limited or dependent upon the response of the one who receives our gift.

In summary, although the rewards are promised, may we seek the simplicity of pleasing the Lord in all that we do, and may His smiling face be our most sought-after reward. "And whatsoever ye do, do it heartily as to the Lord, and not unto men; knowing that of the Lord ye shall receive the reward of the inheritance: for ye serve the Lord Christ" (Col. 3:23-24)

There Is a Second Death

Rev. 20:14

Heavenly Father, we approach Your throne on behalf of those who have not come to know You. In the rush of daily life, it is all too easy to neglect to ponder our eternal fate. We pray that Your Spirit would draw those who have, for whatever reason, ignored Your salvation. May Your word come to them with the power of Your anointing and pierce the veil of unbelief. May the needy turn to You in the midst of distress to find Your compassion and forgiveness. Let Your word go forth to dispel false teachings. Guide our steps in the right way. In Jesus's name we pray. Amen.

Revelation 20:14 speaks of the second death. This raises questions concerning the first death. What is it? Where do we go after we die? Are all people treated equally after death? And then there is the question, "What is the second death?" The fact that there is a second death means that the first death (death as we know it) is not a ceasing to exist. There are events that *every* one of us will experience after death. However, they are not the same for all people. At this point let me clarify that the scripture does not support the false teaching of reincarnation, nor does it support the idea that all go to heaven. What we are speaking about is the judgment of God on all, which takes place after we die, and the state of our souls until that judgment.

The scripture states in Hebrews 9:27, "It is appointed unto men once to die, but after this the judgment." What happens until and after this judgment? Existence continues for all men! The scripture does not tell us of any ceasing to exist, even for those who fall under the wrath of God (the non-believers). We are taught that if our names are written in the Lamb's book of life, we will live forever in heaven with Jesus. (Rev.21:27) Having our name on a church roll is insufficient. Heaven is for those who have had their sins washed away with the blood of Jesus, through faith in Him. If our names are in this book, then upon death we go to be in the presence of the Lord, receiving the reward of our faith (2 Cor. 5:8). The second death has no effect upon us for it does not apply to us. Thus, death for the Christian believer is a passing into the promise of life eternal in the presence of the Lord. This is a glorious event for the blood-washed saints of God! (Rev. 20:6)

What then is the fate of the person who dies without his/her sins forgiven through faith in the redemptive work of Jesus on the cross? The scripture tells us that one thousand years after the Lord's return to earth comes the great judgment of God when every individual will stand before Him. (Rev. 20:12) After this judgment, all those whose names are not written in the book of life pass through the second death. The Bible tells us that on the other side of the second death there is existence. However, it is an existence of eternal torment. As we read in Revelations 21:87, "But the fearful and unbelieving... shall have their part in the lake which burneth with fire and brimstone: which is the second death." The scripture makes it very clear that this second death is not a ceasing to exist as stated in Rev. 14:11, "And the smoke of their torment ascendeth up for ever and ever: and they have no rest day nor night." (See also Luke 16:22-26)

We then are given a say in the eternal state of our existence. If we reject the love of God through Jesus, we are condemned to an existence of eternal torment. To receive the love of God through faith in Jesus is to assure us of life eternal in heaven. Therefore, the second death is not something that we must experience. God gives every soul a choice. While there is much more to being a Christian than assuring ourselves of a place in heaven, it is certainly the cornerstone of our faith.

How then do we assure ourselves that we can escape the second death? The answer is simple and explained clearly in John 3:16-18, "For God so loved the world, that he gave his only begotten Son, that whosoever believeth in him should not perish, but have everlasting life. For God sent not his Son into the world to condemn the world, but that the world through him might be saved. He that believeth on him is not condemned: but he that believeth not is condemned already, because he hath not believed in the name of the only begotten Son of God."

To be sure you are bound for eternal life and not eternal torment, believe that Jesus died for your sins. Believe that His shed blood and sacrificial death on the cross are the atonement and cleansing for your sins. Tell God you are truly sorry for your sins and admit that you are a sinner. Ask Jesus to come into your heart and surrender your life to Him. By His Holy Spirit, you will receive the promise of eternal life and will become what the Bible calls born again. You will be made alive in the Spirit, quickened to eternal life through the power of the Spirit of God, the same power that raised Jesus from the dead.

The choice is yours. Don't pass up the opportunity to secure your place in heaven and avoid the torment of the second death. Jesus loves you. He died for you. He is waiting for you to ask for His forgiveness. It doesn't matter how sinful you have been. The blood of Jesus cleanses all sins, great and small. (1 John 1:7) Ask Jesus into your heart today while you have the opportunity, for no one knows the hour of the Lord's return.

The Divine Process

Ephesians 4:15

Heavenly Father, we come to You for protection and refuge, for many are the forces which seek to deceive. Our enemy comes not looking like darkness, but rather looking like an angel of light. From such a foe we need Your divine protection. Cause us to rest in You and hear the still small voice of the Spirit. May the motivations of the flesh be stilled so that we hear the gentle moving of the Holy Spirit of God. Preserve us unto the day of Your coming. In Jesus's name we pray. Amen.

There is a process by which God's work is accomplished in the heart of an individual. This process is in harmony with God's ultimate intention for those who love Jesus, which is that we might be transformed into His image and reflect His character. This is not a small project! We were born in sin; we are self-willed; we seek our own way and have to battle with our ego. We are easily tempted to take what we learn of God and utilize it in the energies of self and soul, rather than yield them up as tools for the Holy Spirit. Perhaps we lean in this direction because we have not been taught the difference. None-the-less, the process of God working in person's heart is substantial.

We are admonished in the scriptures to "grow up into Him in all things." (Eph. 4:15) Growing takes time. There is no instant drive-up window through which we may go to order up a completed spirituality and maturity in Christ. Nature teaches us that growth takes time. The life stories of the great people of God also show us that growth and preparation for service take time. Let us visit just a few to see what is involved in this divine process of preparation.

Joseph, as a very young man, had a dream or a vision from God. God was revealing what He would do in the future. In Genesis 37 we read of the vision of all of Joseph's family, as well as many others, bowing down to him. Joseph had this vision. It was real. But it was not for many years that it came to pass. And during those years God took Joseph through many different, and sometimes painful, experiences, all the while working in his heart. He was sold by his jealous brothers as a slave and taken to Egypt. (Gen.37:28) He was falsely accused of sexual misconduct with his owner's wife and placed in prison. (Gen. 39:20) He lived many years in exile, raising a family in a foreign land. However, God prospered Joseph greatly until he rose to rule the entire land of Egypt, under Pharaoh. The vision was then fulfilled as God used Joseph to save Jacob's family and prosper His people. (Gen.45)

Moses, as a young man, thought that his people would understand that he would help deliver them from bondage in the land of Egypt. (Acts 7:25) However, it wasn't until forty years later, after he had fled Egypt, married, and raised children, that God finally spoke to him telling him to return to Egypt to deliver His people. (Acts 7 :30)

David also was called. He was anointed king at an early age. (1 Sam. 16:13) However, his path did not lead him straight to the throne, but rather through many difficult and trying years. He served in the army under King Saul, only to be hated and pursued. He ultimately fled his home nation for fear of his life. (1 Sam. 18-30) Once he was made king, it was not over all of Israel, but only over Judah. (2 Sam. 2:4) Through many trying situations and battles, the entire nation was finally under David's rule. (2 Sam. 5:3)

And remember Joshua. He did not one day decide to lead the

nation of Israel into the promised land but was prepared as Moses' servant for forty years in the wilderness. And even then, God had planned to give them the promised land, by little and little until they were increased. (Exodus 23:29-30)

God's work in the heart of a person takes time. There is a divine process tailored to each child of God to prepare that one for God's intention for his life. The process is the cross. The crossing out of the self-will and the learning to yield to God, the quieting of the self-motivated religious servant and the establishing of the follower of the Holy Spirit. There is a subtle counterfeit for the moving of the Holy Spirit. It comes looking and sounding good, pronouncing encouragement to act, and become a doer of great things for God. However, the danger is that the motivation is a force from the soulish level and not the Spirit. It is a false voice that would say "just as Joshua decided to rise up and take the promised land, so must we" without giving appropriate reference to the many years of preparation and God's timing, which are always required for the true work of the Spirit. It is a false voice that would say, "we will take this city (or nation) for our God, in Jesus's name!" While this sounds tremendously exciting and certainly appears to be of faith, in fact it is the voice of man's self-motivation. Nowhere do we find Paul or Peter making such a statement as "we shall take all of Rome for Jesus." scripture states clearly that in the last times darkness will cover the people, and men will turn away from God. (Isaiah 60:2; 2 Thessalonians 2:1-4; 2 Tim. 3:1-8) Not that Jesus will refrain from saving souls, for He will continue to save the lost, but it is soulish motivation at its peak that presumes to "take this world for Jesus." Jesus will take it when He returns!

It is easy to speak only of the great victories in scripture, but we must also preface them by the inner work of God in the hearts, and the divine timing and planning that preceded all such wonderful works. The divine process takes us first to the cross, through the process of dying daily to self. Then wisdom, character, balanced insight and a resting in the Holy Spirit begin to grow, allowing us to follow and not grieve Him. The maturing souls of the believers do not need motivational speakers; they need Holy Spirit teachers. Motivation is a short-lived boost to the mind and emotions. Holy Spirit teaching forms a foundation for continuing strength and victorious living.

We should exercise caution, lest we start work on the tenth floor of the building without proper regard for the foundation and first nine floors. Neither Moses, Joseph, David nor Joshua could have done the works of God one day prior to the Lord's appointed time. Imagine the folly of Joshua telling Moses twenty years into the wilderness (and twenty years prior to God's timing) that he had the faith and vision to lead the people into the promised land, and that it was time to go. Yet certain voices today proclaim just such a faith. We must be careful lest we be swept up in the motivational forces of flesh and deception (veiled as faith and light). Those who move to the voice of soulish motivation will find it very difficult to hear and follow the voice of the Holy Spirit.

In conclusion, Hebrews chapter eleven speaks of the great people of faith outlining many victories, many triumphs and answers to prayer. It concludes with "others were tortured... stoned... slain... afflicted ... tormented." (Hebrews 11:37) And it further states that "all these, having obtained a good report through faith." (Hebrews 11:39) This is Holy Ghost faith. Faith that keeps on going when things are falling down around us! Faith that walks confidently through affliction. Faith that faces all that we may not be able to understand with the confident knowing that God is with His people. Greater than the parting of the sea...greater than the defeating of enemy armies... greater than the healing of a sick body... greater than any other thing is the precious faith of one soul. A faith which allows us to daily trust in Jesus through the midst of trials, suffering and adversity. This is the great work of God, and it is in the heart of individuals.

Because Your Adversary the Devil Walketh About Seeking Whom He May Devour

1 Peter 5:8

Heavenly Father, we come to You as we have many times before, weary and in need of Your refreshing. Many are the pressures which come to burden our souls. Many are the challenges which test our faith. There is much we do not understand. Help us in all things to trust in You. Keep us with a heart to seek You that Your peace may reside within us. Protect us from the condemnation of the devil who would rob us of our joy in the midst of the testing. We claim Your protection and strength as we face that which is before us. Forgive us for our sins, and free us from the guilt associated with our errors and ignorance. We thank You for Your patience and understanding. In Jesus's name we pray. Amen.

The Christian experience is a life-long journey. It is much more than being born again, forgiven of our sins and being bound for eternal life in heaven. Along the way we will have many experiences and challenges. God desires each believer to develop in character and maturity, to be victorious over the challenges of evil, and to conquer the demands of the fallen, self-centered, old nature. As we read in Eph. 4:13, "till we all come... unto the measure of the stature of the fullness of Christ."

Satan is a formidable adversary. He deceives and appears as an angel of light. As we read above, he is seeking. But what is he seeking? We know that his goal is to destroy, but what does he seek to accomplish this goal, and how can we prepare ourselves to not be destroyed? God desires us to be equipped with protection against the enemy. That protection is provided through the word of God. As our understanding is increased, and as our spiritual stature is strengthened, we are less likely to succumb to the onslaught of the devil. Without correct spiritual understanding from the word, we are more vulnerable to defeat.

Satan seeks to destroy by working to activate and direct the flesh-man, the old nature, self-centered person in each of us. This is the person that is to be "crucified with him, that the body of sin might be destroyed, that henceforth we should not serve sin." (Romans 6:6) It is essential that the believer know that yes, Satan is our adversary, but so is our flesh. If we do not recognize this enemy, we are more likely to hinder our progress in God and to aid Satan in his seeking to destroy. In Romans 8, we read of the flesh being the enemy of things spiritual "that the righteousness of the law might be fulfilled in us, who walk not after the flesh, but after the spirit... for to be carnally minded is death; but to be spiritually minded is life and peace. Because the carnal mind is enmity (in opposition and hostile) against God." (Romans 8:4-7) Satan therefore seeks a partnership with our flesh man in order to drive us away from God's purposes. This is what he is seeking: anyone of flesh who will listen to him and yield to his deceptive ways.

We must allow God to put our self-nature to death, through the inner working of the Spirit in our lives, to keep us safe from the enemy. In Romans 6: 11, we read sound advice to assist us in understanding how to remain free from sin and the destroyer. "Likewise reckon ye also yourselves to be dead indeed unto sin, but alive unto God through Jesus Christ our Lord... Let not sin therefore reign in your mortal body." Earlier in Romans 6:3-7 we read of our being dead, crucified and buried with him. This is how we must reckon our self-nature to prevent the enemy from finding a "partner" in us to accomplish destruction.

In Romans seven, we read of the continual struggle between the old flesh and sin, with the spiritual desire for God and the new, born-again person of the spirit. This struggle is continuous as long as we remain in this earthly tabernacle. We must learn this and the key to overcoming. That key is the cross, absent from much that is taught today, but necessary for true and lasting victory over the enemy. We need to learn to submit to the crossing of our wills as God puts to death the self-nature. This process hurts. It is not pleasant, but it is necessary for our own protection. Paul stated, "I die daily." (1 Cor. 15:31) The process of death to self is never over. It can never be forgotten. It is the key to our safety and spiritual maturity. We must learn to embrace the cross (the dying to self and the crossing of our wills) even as did our Lord. His final prayer was (as he was facing the ultimate dying to self) "nevertheless, not as I will, but as thou wilt." (Matt.26:39) Nevertheless is a tremendous word here. scripture is teaching us that our hearts attitude should be, regardless of what I want, and no matter what the result is to me personally, and no matter what it may cost me, and no matter what the pain, Your will be done Oh God, not mine. This is our example to follow. This is the heart attitude that will lead to victory and resurrection power in our lives. This is the attitude that will ren der the destroyer powerless.

To win over the devil, we must win over our own selfishness. If we only think to fight the devil, we miss out in understanding that his target is our other enemy, our own fleshly self. We are in the battleground with fighting waging on two fronts: the devil and the flesh. God is on our side, and the victory is sure, as long as we understand how to win. It takes the power of the Spirit to bring victory. That power is unleashed as the self is put to death and God is enthroned upon our hearts. This is not an easy message to learn. It is not as popular as other less costly approaches to God. Yet it is the scriptural approach

Being His follower does not mean taking the easy way, for the road is uphill to the end and leads to the cross. "If any man will come after me, let him deny himself, and take up his cross, and follow me." (Matt.16:24) Taking up the cross does not mean doing only the spiritual things we enjoy. It means allowing God to take us through life to learn His lessons: maturity, responsibility, integrity, honest, and hard work. It means doing the task at hand to the glory of God, whether that task is pleasant or not, or spiritual or not in our own judgment. It means working for a living, paying our bills on time and not misusing or overextending credit financially. It means providing for a family, supporting and praying for our spouse, nurturing and encouraging our children. It means praying and worshipping day in and day out, in good times, and in trying times. It means living a life pleasing unto God in the common places of life, in private, and in public. It means living a life that is His witness, in a dark world, in the place that we find ourselves. It means trusting in God to provide for the work which He wants done. It means the death of spiritual ego. It means waiting upon God for all things and trusting in His timing. It means loving Jesus and wanting His will more than our own plans for Him or for ourselves. It means following Him, not pulling Him into our own desires.

Oh, Lord, teach us the way of the cross, and help us
discern the difference between our own ambitions and
Your working in us. Keep us safe from ourselves and
the devil's attacks. In Jesus's name we pray. Amen.

The Word and
the Cross

Heavenly Father, most holy God, we come to You and
acknowledge Your majesty and power. The gifts of Your Spirit
are a manifestation of Your glorious Self. They are a holy thing.
They are a part of You. May we know that to be where Your gifts
are operating is to stand upon holy ground. Teach us to discern
Your work and gifts from that of the impostor. May we be kept
in step with Your ways and drawn closer in our relationship with
You, not to be distracted by apparent spiritual things which lack
Your anointing and holiness. In Jesus's name we pray. Amen.

Our relationship with God is fashioned by our understanding of
Him. We need to know Him. We need to understand Him and
know of His ways. This we learn through His word. The application
of truth from His word comes to us through the Holy Spirit. The
Holy Spirit applies the truth to our hearts and minds to cause
us to know Him. We can trust in the application of the word to
our understanding to the degree that we embrace the cross. If we
embrace the cross and yield our wills to God, then the Holy Spirit
applies the word to our understanding. To the degree that we avoid
the cross and yielding our wills to God, we are open to deception
and the improper application of truth. We will understand clearly
to the degree that we embrace the cross.

Our love for Him is in direct response to increasing our knowledge of Him through His word. It is impossible not to love Him as we understand Him. Only the rebellious and self-willed can profess no love for God. The yielded cry out of His great mercy and glory and tell of their adoration toward Him, for they have seen Him as He is through an understanding gained from the word. Our worship of Him is founded properly when our understanding is based upon the truth of His word gained by embracing the living of a crucified life.

All that surrounds the word is peripheral and secondary in importance to gaining an understanding of God. The signs and wonders of God are not nearly as important as the word. God will bear witness to the word if it is correctly taught, to cause the word to be received. Signs and wonders which do not line up with the word, or which accompany teaching and behavior not in line with the word, should be questioned. scripture speaks of deceiving signs and lying wonders done by Satan. (2 Thessalonians 2:9) Where there is spiritual activity with the gifts, yet no teaching of the word and the cross, there is at least improper emphasis, and very likely deception. The gifts cannot be taught. There can be no seminars on how to operate the gifts of the Spirit. Such talk is rooted in misunderstanding. God will follow the correct teaching of the word with the manifestation of the gifts, signs, and wonders. Therefore, signs and wonders are not what we are to seek after, nor what is to be taught. We are to teach the word. We are to seek after the correct teaching of the word and the rest will follow. When the teaching is about the death to self through the work of the cross, the power of God will be present. When one tries to teach about the power of God absent the cross, the wrong power will be present. When one tries to teach about the gifts of the Spirit, the signs, and wonders of God and how to make them appear, then incorrect emphasis invites the wrong power. It is true that we are encouraged to desire spiritual gifts. They are a beautiful and special part of the Christian experience. However, there must be the proper preparation of the heart, or we will be attempting to put new wine in old wine skins.

There is a dire need to teach the word of God, and that there is no substitute for the cross. We need to learn there must be a yielding to God and a death to self before any godly power will be manifest. The power is not what we are to seek after. If we seek to know Him, love Him, and understand His word, He will manifest Himself. It is His word. They are His gifts. The signs and wonders come from His hand. They are the gracious manifestation of God Himself, when He beholds the hearts that are focused upon His word and seeking Him, not His manifestations. We get it all wrong when we seek that which is to follow the word and not the Lord Himself. In Psalms 103:7 we read, "He made known His ways unto Moses, His acts unto the children of Israel." It is His ways that God wishes us to learn. It is a shallower experience to know only His acts. And to seek His acts of themselves is to misunderstand their purpose. They are the extra blessing, the added confirmation, but not the main ingredient. The main ingredient is the *person* of God, and to know Him is the central message.

In Mark 16:20 we read, "And they went forth and preached everywhere, the Lord working with them, and confirming the word with signs following." They did not go forth preaching the signs, the wonders, and the gifts. They went forth teaching the word, and the signs followed. If the signs are not following, we should examine our hearts and seek to better deliver the word. To seek the signs is dangerously out of order. When we get it right with the word, God will do His part to confirm the same.

For Though He Was Crucified Through Weakness

2 Cor. 13:4

Heavenly Father, as we are pressed upon by the things of this world, our vision is sometimes clouded. Darkness seeks to sow the seeds of doubt as we behold the ravages of the battle against sin and evil. We look about and do not always behold victory. But, in You, our victory is sure and the struggles we behold are brief disturbances along the way. Our hope remains in Your resurrection and the promise of Your return. With eternal life as our promise, we do well to not let the day's troubles have more power than they should. When our thoughts are on You and Your kingdom, all else that may touch us is reduced to nothing. Hasten the day of Your return, for we long to greet You and enter fully into that which our hearts have tasted. Teach us the discipline of keeping our eyes upon You, for in doing this our hearts will have peace. In Jesus's name we pray. Amen.

What is this weakness which led Jesus to the cross? How can it be said that the Son of God was weak? As we ponder this statement, we see that the only weakness Jesus had was the body of flesh in which he dwelt, a body which was weak enough to suffer death like all men. As we look beneath the appearance of weakness, we behold a supernatural strength and Godly power. For it took God's power in Jesus to allow Jesus to proceed to the cross when He continued to possess the power to NOT go to the cross.

Jesus knew that the ordained steps of His life would lead to the cross. He beheld the cross knowing what would happen to Him when He got there. With perfect obedience to God's plan, He wavered not from the path but determined to take each step necessary to fulfill dying on the cross to redeem lost man. When Peter tried to defend Jesus in the garden of Gethsemane and drew his sword, Jesus said, "Put up again thy sword into his place... Thinkest thou that I cannot now pray to my Father, and he shall presently give me more than twelve legions of angels? But how then shall the scriptures be fulfilled?" (Matt. 26:52-54) Jesus refused to waver from the path of the cross. Inwardly, He was charged with power to complete the purpose of His coming. In Gethsemane, Jesus saw the suffering He would endure and chose to embrace it. Weakness would not have done so. Jesus didn't run to get the suffering over with, nor did He turn from the path toward it. He took each step and, with determination, obediently took the next. With each step He embraced the will of God and accepted the suffering and shame as the plan of salvation unfolded.

Jesus knew of the victory that was waiting for Him after the cross, for we read in Hebrews 12:2, "Who for the joy that was set before him endured the cross, despising the shame, and is set down at the right hand of the throne of God." We ourselves are given the same promise throughout scripture, as we are promised eternal life and the forgiveness of our sins. We are told to look to Jesus as our example in the times when we may be seeking to avoid the cross as it touches our lives. We read in Hebrews 12:2-3, "Looking unto Jesus the author and finisher of our faith... For consider him that endured such contradiction of sinners against himself, lest ye be wearied and faint in your minds." We are asked to embrace the path of the cross just as Jesus was. And it is through His Spirit within that we find the power to take each step with determination and not waver. As we yield to His will within us, our hearts will say, "I will endure the cross and not turn from it, for I see the joy and glory that lies on the other side of obedience." Jesus shared our weakness in the flesh. He knows and understands our struggles. Through His Spirit we share His power to overcome.

Regardless of the trials and troubles which touch us, we find hope in the truth that Jesus rose from the dead. If He rose from the dead, then we too shall rise from the dead, and anything that happens to us between now and then, let it be to the fulfilling of His will. For what comparison can we make with our troubles, when we place them in the perspective of rising from the dead, to spend eternity with Him, free from our sins. This is the joy set before us. Let us not take our eyes from it. Jesus died, shed His blood to cleanse us of our sins and rose from the dead to proclaim His promise to all believers of eternal life. This should be our focus. This is our hope and promise. This is our source of joy. Why should we spend one moment in sadness of heart when the kingdom of God has been offered to us as our home forever? And why should we waver from the path of the cross, when He has asked us to follow, and the fullness of joy is given as our reward? "And whosoever doth not bear his cross, and come after me, cannot be my disciple." (Luke: 14:27)

The Veil Is Upon Their Heart

2 Cor. 3:15

Heavenly Father, we bring to You our many concerns and heartfelt pains, our tears and innermost longings. Into Your gentle and caring hands, we place our most precious treasures. We have labored to preserve them and are learning that we cannot. We have wearied our souls with cares for things we cannot control. Let the time past be sufficient for not releasing all into Your care, for when we are burdened our life is a blessing to no one. Today, we give all that burdens our hearts to You. Today, we rejoice in Your love. Today, we praise You. Let our time be spent in praise, even when our perceived treasures vanish and we understand not, for You, Lord, are our only true treasure. In Jesus's name we pray. Amen.

In any area of our heart where we resist yielding to the work of the Spirit, a veil remains upon our heart. This veil blinds us from the glory of God's fullness in that area and prevents the glory of the Lord from radiating through our lives. It is a veil that blinds our understanding. God does not want a veil between us and His revelation. He desires us to see and understand. It is our lack of yielding all things to His control that veils us from the truth and way of the Spirit. It is not always easy to yield important things over into the hands of God. We want to stay in control. We want to direct things to our own desired conclusion. We may feel that our desire is God's, but if our actions are motivated from behind the veil where an unyielding self seeks control, we are not abiding in the Spirit, and works of the flesh are the result rather than the work of the Holy Spirit. Much activity of the believer today is from behind the veil. Thus, we see strife, confusion and a lack of authority and power. When God gets us out from the veil, the Spirit will move, and the anointing of the Spirit will flow. When the veil is removed, Jesus is the only focus. While the veil remains, our priorities are ordered in a realm not fully in the Spirit, and our energy is spent in worldly or religious ways rather than in the Spirit. The veil of the temple was torn when Jesus was on the cross. (Matt. 27:51) The veil in our own hearts will also be removed when we come to the cross and yield, from our very core, our will to Him in all things. Behind the veil, one moves in a fleshly realm attempting to accomplish spiritual things. This cannot be done, for the veil is not removed until our will is put to death by the inner work of the cross in our hearts. "But when it shall turn to the Lord, the veil shall be taken away." (2 Cor. 3:16)

If It Be Possible Let This Cup Pass from Me

Matt. 26:39

Heavenly Father, it is a privilege to come once again unto You. You are forever unchanging and a certain place of refuge Who never forsakes us. Your patience and understanding are more than we deserve. Over time, You make known unto us Your ways and for this we are grateful. Through every experience You bring eternal light and understanding to us as we look to You. Things which we once embraced as truth are gently removed and replaced with the greater love and light from Your word. Each day is exciting, Lord, for in it lies the possibility of learning yet more. Help us have teachable spirits and bring us into the fullness of living in the Spirit. In Jesus's name we pray. Amen.

The Bibles says we are to take up our cross and follow Jesus. To grasp a portion of the meaning of this, let us look at our Savior as He faced His cross. As He prayed in the garden of Gethsemane, knowing that very soon He would be taken and crucified, He looked at that which was terrible beyond our comprehension. The very Son of God looked at His cross and prayed to the Father, "O my Father, if it be possible, let this cup pass from me." (Matt. 26:39) What he beheld was foreign to His life. It would take His life. His flesh cried out for it to be removed for He did not like it. He would not have been found praying thus if he liked what was before Him. He did not like it. Then, with godly determination He added to His prayer, "nevertheless not as I will, but as thou wilt." (Matt. 26:39) He of Himself would have willed for it to be removed, but His inner spirit and commitment to God drove Him to yield to the Father's will. Jesus is found praying this not once, but three times before He had the matter settled. This tells us of the great consternation taking place within Him in these moments of facing the reality of the cross.

We do not always understand the work of the Spirit in our hearts. Often what God presents is foreign to our thinking. Often, we do not like what we see coming or are asked to do. If we can accept the truth that the cross, and God's work in the heart, do not always feel good or comfortable, then we are postured for growth. With growth comes blessing, but before blessing comes obedience to God. When something shatters our preconceived ideas, overturns our desires, or hurts, the chances are it is good for us. We find this same principle in the parable of the corn of wheat as we read in John 12:24, "Except a corn of wheat fall into the ground and die, it abideth alone: but if it die, it bringeth forth much fruit."

Discernment is necessary to tell the difference between yielding to the work of the cross and placing religious garments upon an unyielded self. It is easier to do the latter, but the results are poor. Paul, before his conversion, was full of religious activities and clothed with a marvelous religious pedigree. All the while however, he was fighting Jesus instead of yielding to Him. The Pharisees were clothed with many religious deeds and actions, so much so that Jesus called them whited sepulchers, which appeared outwardly wonderful but inside were full of dead men's bones.

A simple example of the difference is told us in Luke 18:10-14, "Two men went up into the temple to pray; the one a Pharisee, and the other a publican. The Pharisee stood and prayed thus with himself, "God, I thank thee, that I am not as other men are, extortioners, unjust, adulterers, or even as this publican. I fast twice in the week, I give tithes of all that I possess." And the publican, standing afar off, would not lift up so much as his eyes unto heaven, but smote upon his breast, saying, "God be merciful to me a sinner." I tell you, this man went down to his house justified rather than the other: for every one that exalteth himself shall be abased; and he that humbleth himself shall be exalted." In this story, the religious and apparent sacrificial activity of prayer, fasting, and tithing were resulting in the Pharisee exalting himself in his own eyes. This sacrificial activity was not the work of the cross, or the Spirit, in his heart. He took these things upon himself to clothe himself with religious activities without ever yielding the heart properly to the Lord. On the other hand, the publican came with no works to boast of, no grand sacrificial activities, and fell before God humbly asking for mercy, realizing his true state. God then takes upon Himself to clothe this publican with justification. Our works are of no value in bettering ourselves in the sight of God. It is the heart attitude that God seeks to make right.

The results of the work of God in the heart lead to a state of being in Him, not doing things alone. Our thinking and actions are changed from the inside as we yield to God, not clothed from the outside with religious activities. We become in our existence and expressions more like Jesus. We are more loving, more patient, more forgiving, more compassionate in all of our life, as Jesus takes us through the cross as He intends. All the sacrifices we can possibly make are worthless without this inner changing as a result of the Spirit's work. (1 Cor.13) As we abide in Him, all that we do in life becomes a sweet savor unto God, from the simplest ordinary task to the precious moments of worship. Without this right heart attitude even the greatest of sacrifices is not accepted or of benefit. Psalms 51:16-17 says it well, "For thou desirest not sacrifice; else would I give it: thou delightest not in burnt offering. The sacrifices of God are a broken spirit: a broken and a contrite heart, 0 God, thou wilt not despise."

We cannot make our own cross to bear. We cannot make

uncalled for religious sacrifices to hasten our growth. In all that we live through, the common and the divine, we shall bear the fruit of the Spirit more fully to the benefit of all, as we learn to rest in Jesus and trust Him to accomplish His good work in our hearts. The Pharisee may have appeared to all to be far ahead of the publican, but in God's eyes his accomplishments were a hindrance. While the Pharisee may have thought himself a blessing to others, the publican was more likely used of the Spirit (though unaware to him) because of a proper heart attitude. We bear fruit because of the inner work of the Spirit, not because of our works. We should stay clear of the error which thinks that works of themselves are pleasing to God. Unless born of the Spirit of God from within, they are no more pleasing in us than they were in the Pharisee. The work of the cross is not measured by works, but by the fruits of the Spirit. "But the fruit of the Spirit is love, joy, peace, longsuffering, gentleness, goodness, faith, meekness, temperance." (Gal. 522-23) It is to the fruit of the Spirit that others are drawn, and thus drawn to Jesus. Sacrifices and religious works which are not born of the Spirit are as a fruitful tree painted on a wall. They may look good and be accomplished quickly, but they are of no use to the passers-by. Fruit of the Spirit, which is the result of the work of the cross in the heart, is like an orchard of fruitful trees bearing nourishing fruit to all who come near. It takes years for a tree to develop fruitfulness, whereas a painted wall can look good in a day. May God grant us the grace to yield to His precious work and discern the difference between our premature, self-motivated actions and sacrifices, and the true work of the Spirit. Grant Lord, that Your fruitfulness may abound with in us to the benefit of those around us.

He Hath Not Dealt
with Us After Our Sins

Psalm 103:10

Our Father and our Savior, to You we are grateful. Your love
and acceptance are a free and undeserved gift. Let us not grieve
You by hesitating to accept gladly that which You greatly desire
us to have. May we be given grace to keep our eyes upon You,
and Your love for us, in the midst of all that may touch our
lives. You knew of our imperfections long before saving us.
They did not stand in Your way when You first saved us. May
they not hinder our relationship with You now by our focusing
on them instead of You. We worship You and thank You for
Your unconditional love. In Jesus's name we pray. Amen.

As we journey through this life, we experience many different
circumstances. Some of them we seem to understand while some
leave us wondering. When good things happen to us, we relate
them to God's love for us and feel comforted, associating the good
things with a feeling that God is pleased. When trials, testing or
hardship touch our life, it is easy to feel that God is moving away
from us and that the bad which has come is the result of our sin
or error in the sight of God. Because we realize that we fall short
of the perfection and righteousness of God, it is easy to accept

condemnation; particularly when we do not understand the why of our circumstances. This is certainly not God's intention. When we accept condemnation and thoughts of uselessness, Satan has succeeded in disabling a servant of the Lord. When our eyes are upon our own failures or shortcomings, we tend to listen to Satan's condemnation, and it seems to fit. We must remember that it is those very shortcomings that Jesus saw and died for. They are covered in His blood and washed away. God's love is not determined by our circumstances. His love is constant and unchanging whether we are in good or bad situations. The process of perfecting us may not be complete, but there is no condemnation to those who are in Christ Jesus.

Truth is a wonderfully freeing power. Yes, we are of ourselves worthless. Yes, we deserve condemnation. Yes, of ourselves we are useless to God. It is all true! But the greater truth is that because of all of this, Jesus shed His precious blood to wash us of our sins and make us worthy in the sight of God. This is the power of God and gift of God to all who believe in Jesus. We may fail a thousand times and stumble even more, but not one such failure changes the love God has toward us nor the power of His word. We may seek a safe harbor from the storm of thoughts that seek to drive us from trusting in and accepting God's love, but the winds will cease, and the storm become quiet the moment we place our eyes upon Jesus and once again embrace His word as true, accepting it as His gift to us.

Psalm 103:10-14 says it so beautifully, "He hath not dealt with us after our sins; nor rewarded us according to our iniquities. For as the heaven is high above the earth, so great is his mercy toward them that fear him. As far as the east is from the west, so far hath he removed our transgressions from us. Like as a father pitieth his children, so the Lord pitieth them that fear him. For He knoweth our frame, he remembereth that we are dust." These words cannot be improved upon. He has not given us what we deserve because of our sins, but rather has had mercy upon us. He has taken our sins and cast them far away. He knows our frame, our sins, our weakness, and faults, and yet comes to us through Jesus to bless us and draw us unto Himself. Condemnation does not fit into the context of God's expression of love toward us.

Satan cannot rob us of our peace in God unless we allow thoughts born of darkness and lies to dwell in our hearts and minds. The mind truly is a battlefield and 1 Peter 1:13 states it very well, "Gird up the loins of your mind, be sober, and hope to the end for the grace that is to be brought unto you at the revelation of Jesus Christ." We are not to allow any interruption in our hope in God's promises and love toward us. We are to hold our hope in His word until the very end. Condemnation seeks to break our hope connection with God and send us into a joyless, powerless, useless life. We are not to let the enemy succeed.

Our worthiness and usefulness to God is not conditioned upon religious activity, church membership, or the acceptance of man. In fact, such measurements can provide a false feeling of comfort based upon man's opinion rather than faith in God. Jesus would have found it difficult to feel worthy by relying upon the opinions of man. One day the opinion would have made Him King, and shortly thereafter it was calling for His death.

Jesus's words in John 16:12 have a good chance of applying to each of us in those things which we do not clearly understand, "I have yet many things to say unto you, but ye cannot bear them now." Let us find rest from the tormenting storm by placing in the hands of God those things which we cannot understand, and never let Satan get his hands on our trust and acceptance of God's love and mercy toward us. Let us remember that "He hath not dealt with us after our sins; nor rewarded us according to our iniquities." (Psalm 103:10) Praise God!

Predestined

Romans 8:30

Father God, the depth of Your word is amazing! As we are shown new glimpses of understanding, we realize that we only scratch the surface of the great truths of God. Even as man walks upon the surface of the earth but cannot clearly see to its core, so we walk in the shallows of all that lies beneath the sacred pages of scripture. Take our hearts and minds and reveal more of Yourself unto us. Thank You for the Holy Spirit, which gives us deeper understanding as we yield our hearts to You. Take us as deep as we are capable of going, for it is our desire to learn more. In Jesus's name we pray. Amen.

Christian living is not a haphazard experience. If I have no purpose in my life, then I dwell in a terrible state of existence. When I have a goal or objective to accomplish, then value and meaning are added to my life. God is a God of purpose. He does not gamble with my destiny. He wants me to understand His purpose for my life. I face the challenge of trying to figure out His plan for my life. God will not keep it a secret from me if I take the time to look. He is merciful and gracious and stands anxious to help.

I must expand the horizons of my thinking to begin to grasp God's plan. Being human and living on this planet we call earth; I tend to relate everything to my earthly experience. I want to know what God's plan is for my life, as I call it. My life being the days I have to live on earth. This is at least what occupies much of my contemplation. God, however, is thinking in terms of eternity, with His plan of eternal life! For me to grasp His intentions, I too must begin to think in terms of eternity. As I lift my eyes past the earthly experience and into the ages beyond, then, and only then, do I set my mind in the proper state to grasp some of God's wonderful intentions. Too often, I tend to think of this life as the after-graduation experience. As a student anxiously awaits graduation from school to begin his own life, so I look for that day on earth when I will step into my purpose. God is looking far past my purpose in this life to fulfill His purpose for me as it relates to eternity.

What is His purpose? What has He planned? A good place to start looking is where scripture speaks of being predestined. These are the things that God has predetermined or planned for us in advance. These are His interests in accomplishing His purpose for me and for you. Somewhere, before time began, God set out a goal for me and you. He planned that we would come to this ultimate purpose as the ages unfolded. He then set the machinery in motion to bring us to that predetermined goal. "For whom he did foreknow, he also did predestinate to be conformed to the image of his Son." (Rom. 8:30) God plans for each of us to be made into the image of Jesus. This is a personal, individual goal for each believer. This intention of God reaches beyond what we may accomplish or not accomplish in this world. This purpose of God is the making of godly men and women. It is the building of integrity, compassion, and strength of character. The school we are enrolled in is called planet earth. Every moment of every day has a purpose in God bringing me and you to the day of graduation; that day when the body shall rest and return to the earth, and our eternal soul will rise to be with the Lord forever.

God's eternal purpose is different from any ministry or work we may be given to do while in this school. Ephesians 2:10 states, "For we are his workmanship, created in Christ Jesus unto good works, which God hath before ordained that we should walk in them." As part of our schooling, we are to walk in good works that are pre ordained by God. This, however, is not God's eternal purpose. This is His earthly purpose for us. The works of ministry, of giving, of praying, and of allowing the gifts of the Spirit to operate are all good works ordained by God. Through them we learn and are prepared, little by little, for His eternal purpose, the image of Jesus.

The trials and stresses of life, the struggles and daily challenges we face, the heartbreaks and the victories are all part of God's hand at work in my life and in your life. If we focus only on the planet earth experiences, we may become discouraged and confused, for they vary depending upon the eternal work God is seeking to accomplish. As a builder uses many different tools to accomplish his goal, and a painter uses many different colors to produce his masterpiece, so God uses many different experiences to move us toward His ultimate predestined purpose for our lives. Some of the names on God's tools could be suffering, adversity, sickness, hardship, victory, and blessing.

Ephesians speaks more about our predetermined destiny in God. We are predestined to be His adopted children. (Eph. 1:5) We are not orphans for all eternity! Though our earthly parents die, yet we are not without God as our Father. We have been adopted by Jesus Christ into the eternal, loving, glorious family of God. In Verse 11, we are told that it is predetermined that we receive an inheritance. This is no meager portion either! We have an eternal inheritance in the riches and glories of the Creator of all things. Not only are we adopted and saved from orphanhood, but we have been chosen by a very wealthy and prosperous Father. Glory to God! The thought of receiving an inheritance of substantial wealth is quite exciting. We envision how our life would change, what we would do with the money, and how happy we would be. How much more we have to be thankful for, as we realize that our des tiny includes an inheritance of wealth beyond our wildest dreams. We have been adopted into a family that was not accessible to us until we were saved from our sins by the great love of God.

As wonderful as this life is at times, particularly when in the blessed presence of the Spirit of God, there is yet a scripture that speaks to the far greater blessedness of what is to come in the vast and endless ages of eternity. In Romans 13: 12, we are told that we are in the night of our experience, and that the day is soon to dawn. Paul likewise explained that now we see through a glass darkly, but then shall we see face to face and know as we are known (1 Cor.13:12). In the night, before the sun rises, objects are not very clear. We see shadows, shapes, and broad generalities, but the details escape us. Colors are muted or non-distinguishable. We cannot fully enjoy the landscape of our surroundings for there is not enough light. Then comes the sun. Suddenly, we see shapes clearly. Colors that previously were darkened burst to life. The cool of the night is dispelled with the warmth of the sun's rays. Day has arrived! What a glorious thought to realize that this is our nighttime experience, and the day is soon to dawn. Soon the rays of the Son of God will brighten our existence and we will see colors, shapes, and a landscape of glory of which, heretofore, we have only had a glimpse.

What glorious love God has for us! He sent His Son, Jesus, to die on the cross, shed His blood for our atonement, and rise from the dead as the firstborn of many into eternal life. This love, shown to us through Jesus, is the love that predestined us to be His children and share in the inheritance of His riches for all eternity. It is in this life that He seeks to prepare us for our destiny! It is coming, and He wants us prepared. Children who inherit great wealth, but have no strength of character, are often destroyed by the power of what they receive. God intends for the Christian to be prepared for his destiny and have the character of Christ, to be able to fully enjoy the inheritance. He knows just what each of us needs to experience to be fitted for this plan. As we learn to lift our eyes to the horizons of God's predetermined purpose, we will receive the strength to endure all the work taking place in our lives. As Paul put it, "Our conversation (citizenship) is in heaven." (Phil 3:20)

Our efforts should be focused upon obtaining God's purpose, not our own. Paul explained that his goal was to seize and possess that which God purposed for him in Christ Jesus. Because this was his focus, what befell him in this life was of little importance to Paul. He pressed on to reach the fullness of the high calling of God in his life. He sought to align himself with the eternal purposes of God. As we seek to do the same, all of heaven will move to help us. When we seek to move into that which God has predetermined, we move into the flow of eternity and a taste of our glorious inheritance. His goal is to make us more like Jesus. (Phil. 3: 12-13)

Yielding Yet More

Heavenly Father, purge us of all remnants of the flesh, and self-will, which plague us and keep us from a deeper relationship with You. Purify our motives in the deep and secret places of the heart. Let us obey the Holy Spirit in every moment of life, and quickly restore us when we stumble over our old man of sin. Kindle a fire of diligence and obedience within our hearts that we may please You. Glorify Your name in the earth and grant us the determination and strength to pay the price of obedience. In Jesus name we pray. Amen.

Who Made Me A Judge or A Divider Over You? (Luke 12:14)

In Luke 12, Jesus was approached by a man with a request for help. He had a situation which, to him, seemed unfair. His brother had received control over an inheritance to which this man thought he had a rightful share. What a shock it must have been when his brother gained control over the inheritance and would not share it. No wonder he felt to seek the help of the Lord in this matter. We know how we would feel if someone took something of ours, something we had every right to have, and robbed us of our ability to possess or have it.

If we unfairly lost money, a source of income, a piece of real estate, a car, or other items which were ours, we too might seek God's intervention in the matter. So, we read, "And one of the company said unto him, Master, speak to my brother, that he divide the inheritance with me," (Luke 12: 13) If this was our request, we would hope and expect the Lord to go with us to our brother and straighten him out. But this was not the Lord's response. Jesus said to him, "Man, who made me a judge or a divider over you?" (Luke 12: 14) This was probably a great shock to the man. Was Jesus supporting a seemingly greedy brothers' action? While the oldest brother, in the culture of that time, did normally receive a greater inheritance, to us today this can seem very unfair.

Such a response would, and should, stop us cold to consider what is wrong. "Why is God so harsh toward me when I feel I am within my rights? Those things I asked for should be mine. What is going on here anyway?" Jesus was speaking the only way he could to this man, because the man's inner heart attitude toward the inheritance was incorrect. He had not yielded the matter to God, but rather was seeking God to help him in his own effort to keep something he did not want to lose. The man's heart was coveting after the inheritance. Perhaps part of it was due him. And yes, his brother may have been wrong to not share it. However, Jesus was working in this man's heart to perfect the inner person of the Spirit. Jesus wants every corner of the believer's heart to be yielded to Him, and He uses all of life's experiences to accomplish that work.

The scripture tells us that "ye are not your own. For ye are bought with a price: therefore, glorify God in your body, and in your spirit, which are God's," (1 Cor. 6:19- 20) If we are not our own, then nothing we may possess in this life is ours either. We must learn to yield all things to Him to receive His blessings. Our reward is not in seeking self-rights, but in yielding self-rights to God and trusting Him for our blessing and reward. This is not easy, but it is necessary if we wish to receive His blessings. If we seek to use the name of the Lord to protect our self-rights, then we misunderstand His Lordship and have fallen into being controlled by the flesh and the devil. In 1 Cor. 6:7, Paul says to those who were going to the law to get matters settled for their own self rights, "Now therefore there is utterly a fault among you, because ye go to law one with another. Why do ye not rather take wrong? why do ye not rather suffer yourselves to be defrauded?" Peter reinforces the same heart attitude in 1 Peter 2:19-23, saying that Jesus committed himself to God when mistreated, trusting God to deal with the offender and the offended. Standing up for ourselves is a heart attitude that is difficult to let go of, but one we must learn to yield to the Spirit's control.

Jesus then, following this man's errant request for recovery of the inheritance, brought forth several teachings on covetousness. By the time He got through, this man must have felt about three inches tall, and had hopefully repented of a wrong heart attitude. Jesus taught that it was foolish to be rich in this world, but not rich toward God. This man was seeking to maintain his worldly riches, but Jesus saw that he was lacking in spiritual riches. (Luke 12:16-21) Scripture teaches that when God is sought first, and the heart is yielding all things to Him, that God would provide and add to a person's life all the blessings that the world is busy seeking. (Luke 12:22-32) God would have given the man who lost a portion of the inheritance much more, had the man placed obedience to God first, yielded his painful losses to heaven's control, and pressed on with his walk with Jesus. (Mark 10:30)

Jesus gives an insightful warning in Luke 12:58, saying, "when thou goest with thine adversary to the magistrate, as thou art in the way, give diligence that thou mayest be delivered from him; lest he hale thee to the judge, and the judge deliver thee to the officer, and the officer cast thee into prison." In other words, when our flesh, self-will, and seeking self-rights (our adversary, and the adversary of the Holy Spirit) seeks to gain control of our hearts and actions, we are best served to quickly seek deliverance from such wrong thinking or we will be cast into the prison of our own self-controlled darkness, until we repent and seek God's help and forgiveness. The Bible teaches us that vengeance belongs to the Lord, and that He will repay, as written in Romans 12: 19: "Dearly beloved, avenge not yourselves [don't seek self-rights], but rather give place unto wrath: for it is written, Vengeance is mine; I will repay, saith the Lord." He continues with an admonition to not be all caught up in anger toward those who wrong us or take from us, for in so doing we would be overcome with evil ourselves, the evil of a wrong and vengeful heart. "Therefore, if thine enemy hunger, feed him; if he thirst, give him drink: for in so doing thou shalt heap coals of fire on his head. Be not overcome of evil but overcome evil with good." (Romans 12:20-21)

And now we can see why Jesus responded as He did. The wronged man should have prayed, "Lord, You see what my brother has done. I come to You and lift the matter into Your hands. Inheritance or not, I am here to serve You and live for You. Make my heart right in this matter and draw my brother closer to You. Keep me from coveting after worldly things and help me release control of this and all things into Your hands. Forgive me for any wrong, bitter, or angry thoughts toward my brother. Thank You that You are my provision and source of life and blessing." May we be granted grace to learn to respond in ways pleasing to God in all matters, and to quickly turn from the adversary of the flesh that would tell us, with Satan's prompting, to take matters into our own hands. Jesus seeks to empty us of self so that our lives may be an even brighter light in this world. As we learn to yield to the Spirit in all of the secret areas of the heart, then we will become as Jesus spoke in Luke 11:36: "If thy whole body therefore be full of light, having no part dark, [no self-seeking left] the whole shall be full of light, as when the bright shining of a candle doth give thee light."

Avoiding The Unpleasant...Why It Doesn't Work!

Heavenly Father, we bow before You with grateful hearts. We take this moment to thank You for Your love and mercy which has so graciously given us the gift of life. Our sins are forgiven and washed completely by the blood· of Jesus. Our hope is renewed daily in the face of every challenge. While fear and uncertainty may flood the hearts of many, yet we stand sure in our trust in You and the promises of Your word. words cannot tell how thankful we are to be known by You and called to be Your children. May we learn to praise and thank You even more for Your great love toward us. In Jesus's name we pray. Amen.

Jesus Prevented Him (Matt. 17 :25)

As we live our lives in this world, we are often faced with a moral dilemma, an ethical challenge, or some situation which will test our character and spiritual convictions. We will be called upon to give an answer, or make a decision regarding a matter which our Lord is observing. We may not consciously consider that He is watching, but He always watches. Peter faced just such a moment when he was questioned, "Doth not your master pay tribute?" (Matt. 17 :24) Peter didn't know quite how to handle the question. He quickly said yes and dismissed the matter.

Peter did not wish to deal with the responsibility of paying tribute and presumed an answer of yes would avoid any difficulty. He would quickly learn that seeking to avoid an issue does not work, particularly with those upon whom the Lord has placed His hand.

When Peter then entered the house where Jesus was, Jesus stopped him and asked a question about tribute and custom. We read, "And when he was come into the house, Jesus prevented him, saying, "what thinkest thou, Simon? Of whom do the kings of the earth take custom or tribute: of their own children, or of strangers?" (Matt. 18:25) There it was again! The issue which Peter had just dismissed moments earlier was brought before his face again, by the Lord. Jesus had observed Peters actions, had found them needing some instruction and improvement, and had immediately brought the matter up with Peter. The Lord will prevent us from moving forward from issues He brings before us until we learn what God desires. He will bring them before us repeatedly, until we listen to His instruction and take the appropriate action.

Following Jesus's preventing Peter, the Lord required Peter to go out and take the necessary action to correct the situation. He required Peter to do the thing which he should have done in the first place, and that was to pay the tribute. We read, "Notwithstanding, lest we should offend them, go thou to the sea, and cast an hook, and take up the fish that first comes up; and when thou hast opened his mouth, thou shalt find a piece of money: that take and give unto them for me and thee." (Matt. 17:27) It would have been easier for Peter to pay the first time. Often, if we mishandle something once, there is more involved in correcting our actions the second time; a walk to the sea, time spent fishing, and then paying the tribute. Seeking to avoid matters which God intends for us to handle only complicates the ultimate solution.

And then there is the lesson of faith, which the Lord packaged into Peter's instructions. A fish's mouth is not normally where one would look to pay a debt. With somewhat of a sense of humor, Jesus teaches Peter to do the right thing, don't avoid responsibility, and God will make a way for you and provide for you. And He did.

Is there a place where we find Jesus preventing us? Standing in the way and calling our attention to a matter we need to address? If so, we are wise to deal with it quickly, as procrastination will only make things more difficult. As we step in the direction of doing the right thing in the sight of God, we can trust in His help, provision, and strength.

I Will Stand (Song Lyrics by Lex Adams)
I will stand,
Though the winds may blow o'er my soul, I will stand and know that His power,
Is greater than
Anything, that comes against me, and that in Him is my victory.
I will put my trust in Him
As my faith is purified, by the fire of the trials that come.
I will stand, and see His love,
I will stand and see His salvation.
I will praise His holy name, When I cannot see the way,
For I know, that by faith I stand and that I am loved by Him
Who died, Who died, for me.
I will see His salvation, See His salvation,
As I stand, He will come,
And I will know His love.

Praise Him Continually and Be Blessed!

Heavenly Father, we pause to take time to praise and thank You. Too often we plead our case before You, are blessed by Your answer and help, and neglect to offer the praise and thanksgiving due You. May we no longer neglect to continue to praise and thank you for all things. Your kindness toward us is unceasing. Your blessings abound in our lives. And through each and every challenge You have kept us, taught us, and led us to a place of greater understanding and peace. Praise and bless Your holy name today and forever! In Jesus name we pray. Amen.

Oh, That Men Would Praise the Lord for His Goodness (Psalms 107:15)

Psalm 107:43 ends with, "Who so is wise, and will observe these things, even they shall understand the lovingkindness of the Lord." Let us look at the messages in this Psalm, that we may be encouraged by God's loving help toward people with many faults and problems such as our own and learn of the Lord's ways and lovingkindness. The first seven verses tell of a time when God's people wandered in the wilderness alone, finding no city in which to dwell. They were hungry, thirsty, and discouraged. We read "...their soul fainted in them. Then they cried unto the Lord in their trouble, and he delivered them out of their distresses. He led them forth by the right way, that they might have a city of habitation." (Psalm 107:5-7) He heard them, and His lovingkindness moved Him to help them when they called. In our challenges, as we call upon the Lord, He will likewise help us. The psalmist then writes in Psalm 107:8, "Oh that men would praise the Lord for his good ness, and for his wonderful works to the children of men!"

Psalm 107:9-14 speaks of the Lord "satisfying the longing soul" and "filling the hungry soul with goodness." Those who were in great affliction because of rebellion toward God, even those He showed mercy and "brought out of the darkness and the shadow of death and break their bands in sunder." (Psalm 109:14) He saved even the rebellious out of distress when they cried unto Him. We may have many flaws and weaknesses, yet as we bring them to Jesus and ask His help, He will not refuse to answer our prayers. He will not stop helping us because of our imperfection. He will help us in our imperfection, as we acknowledge it and call upon His name. The Psalmist then repeats, "Oh that men would praise the Lord for his goodness, and for his wonderful works to the children of men." (Psalm 107:31)

Verses 16-20 speak of fools being in affliction because of their transgressions and coming near to death because of their sin. Yet when they cried unto the Lord He sent and delivered them from their destructions. It is comforting to see that foolish actions or words do not permanently cut us off from the Lord's help. (The Lord knows we have all made enough of them!) Again, we read the repeated message, "Oh that men would praise the Lord for his goodness, and for his wonderful works to the children of men!" (Psalm 107:31)

We then read of those who make a living at sea, in the great ships. David says that these men know the works of God firsthand. We read, "For he commandeth, and raiseth the stormy wind, which lifteth up the waves thereof. They reel to-and-fro, and stagger like a drunken man, and are at their wits end. Then they cry unto the

Lord in their trouble, and he bringeth them out of their distresses. He maketh the storm a calm, so that the waves thereof are still. Then are they glad because they be quiet; so, he bringeth them unto their desired haven." (Psalm 107:25-30) Our storms may not be at sea, but they may be just as distressing. He is with us in them in whatever form they may take. This example is followed again by, "Oh that men would praise the Lord for his goodness, and for his wonderful works to the children of men!" (Psalm 107:31)

David then continues to extol the greatness and kindness of God saying, "He turneth rivers into a wilderness, and the water springs into dry ground; a fruitful land into barrenness, for the wickedness of them that dwell therein." (Psalm 107:33-34) God has power to humble the wicked and proud in many ways, including altering our surroundings, and not through nature alone. We then read, "He turneth the wilderness into a standing water, and dry ground into water springs. And there he maketh the hungry to dwell, that they may prepare a city for habitation; and sow the fields, and plant vineyards, which may yield fruits of increase. He blesseth them also, so that they are multiplied greatly; and suffereth not their cattle to decrease." (Psalm 107:35-38) God makes a way when there seems to be none! He takes the needy, the hungry, the foolish, the rebellious, the distressed, and all others who cry unto Him, and blesses them. He overlooks the weakness and faults of our lives and hears only our cry. Wherever we have been, when we stop and turn to call upon God, in the name of Jesus, His lovingkindness will move Him to help! How glorious!

In every example which David wrote, God came to help and deliver those who called upon Him. And four times David pleaded, "Oh that men would praise the Lord for his goodness, and for his wonderful works to the children of men!" (Psalm 107:31) We cry unto the Lord often and with great effort when we are distressed. He answers in His lovingkindness and mercy. However, do we continue to praise Him and thank Him unceasingly for His goodness and His works of kindness toward us? It is the plea of this psalm that we would. For it is in praise and gratefulness that we are drawn nearer to Him. It is in praise and thanksgiving that we grow in His likeness and are positively influenced by His Spirit. Of the ten lepers healed by Jesus, in Luke 17:11-19, only one returned to praise and glorify God. David observed something similar, for he pleaded repeatedly that men would learn to praise and thank God for His goodness and His works toward men. If we taste of wisdom and understand the lovingkindness of God, we cannot help but praise and thank Him continually. It is in learning to praise Him when blessed, as well as when challenged that we find the richest blessings of God upon our hearts.

Envy...Recognize It! Avoid it!

Heavenly Father, we seek to have Your mind in all things.
Our thinking needs a complete overhaul in so many areas.
Wash us and free us from the limited perception of our
own minds and renew our thoughts with the light of Your
understanding. As we see things the way You see them, then
we find peace, victory, and endurance. Our assurance of Your
nearness comes not from the removal of difficulty, but from
Your insight enlightening our thinking. As we trust in You
and learn Your purposes, then we can rejoice in Your presence
always and in all things. We are grateful and thankful for Your
Spirit, Your love, and Your constant never ceasing care for
us. Thank You that we are loved by Him who died for us and
rose again for our salvation. In Jesus's name we pray. Amen.

Truly God Is Good to Israel (Psalm 73:1)

David speaks of a great enlightenment to his thinking in Psalm 73.
He says, "Truly God is good to Israel, even to such as are of a clean
heart." (Psalm 73:1) This was what he learned- that truly God is
good to His people, even though at times things may appear out of
balance. David acknowledges that his thinking was affected wrongly
by what he perceived to be the inequity of God. Things which David

beheld were "out of balance" in his mind. God was blessing the wicked while harassing the righteous, or so David thought. David says, "For I was envious at the foolish, when I saw the prosperity of the wicked... they are not in trouble as other men; neither are they plagued like other men" (Psalm 73:2-5). This observation was troubling to David, for in his own life he was constantly challenged, chastened, and under the corrective hand of God. He says in Psalm 73:14, "For all the day long have I been plagued and chastened every morning." David saw the foolish and wicked appearing to prosper with a free hand and no correction from God, while he was constantly (every morning) being chastened by the Lord. It seemed wrong, out of balance, unfair. Attempting to understand this apparent inequity was painful for David, it tormented him. (Psalm 73:16.)

In Verse 2, David realized that such thinking was dangerous to his walk and standing with God. He learned that this type of thinking would cause him to slip and fall. Fall into what? Into bitterness of heart, resentment harbored inside that would poison all of David's actions, his witness and his ministry. We need to guard our hearts from any inner seeds of envy, anger, bitterness, or resentment, for they will cut us off from seeing God and understanding His ways. This is Satan's ploy to damage the Christian, for it is we who suffer from wrong heart attitudes, not those of whom we are envious or hold bitterness toward. It is never what happens to us, or what we see happening in the lives of others that is important, it is our inner heart attitude that God seeks to correct and perfect. When David drew near to God and consulted with the Lord, then he learned to think correctly on these matters. We read in Psalm 73:17, "Until I went into the sanctuary of God; then understood I their end." Where there is no chastening from the Lord, there is the development of evil thinking and attitudes. Left untended, wickedness grows like weeds in a garden. Chastening purges the unwanted weeds and prunes the growth of the good plants. Verse 5 states that the wicked were not in trouble as other men. Psalm 73:6-9 explains the results of such apparent ease: "Therefore pride compasseth them about as a chain; violence covereth them as a garment. Their eyes stand out with fatness: they have more than heart could wish. They are corrupt and speak wickedly concerning oppression: they speak loftily. They set their mouth against the heavens, and their tongue walketh through the earth." Left to themselves, they continue in a path of wickedness and darkness. They may appear to prosper, but only for the moment, for as David explains, their end is not pleasant. David saw their ultimate failure and wrote, "Surely thou didst set them in slippery places: thou castedst them down into destruction. How are they brought into desolation, as in a moment! They are utterly consumed with terrors. As a dream when one awaketh; so, O Lord, when thou awakest, thou shalt despise their image." (Psalm 73:18-20)

The wickedness of man is purged by the chastening hand of God. Where there is no chastening, there is no growth and no increase of light. Psalm 73 is David's realization of what we read in Hebrews 12:5-8: "My son, despise not thou the chastening of the Lord, nor faint when thou art rebuked of him: for whom the Lord loveth he chasteneth, and scourgeth every son whom he receiveth. If ye endure chastening, God dealeth with you as with sons; for what son is he whom the father chasteneth not? But if ye be without chastisement, whereof all are partakers, then are ye bastards, and not sons." Prosperity without the chastisement of God may appear good, but it is empty and only a temporary step on the road to destruction.

Prior to understanding these things, David entertained the thought, "Verily I have cleansed my heart in vain" (Psalm 73:13), as he watched the wicked proceed unscathed. It didn't seem fair to David. He was seeking to please God, and yet watched as others who rejected God's ways seemed to prosper and never suffer unfairly. At times, David was challenged, not because of any wrongdoing on his part but by God's allowing things which would help in his growth. We read in Psalm 59 of David being threatened by evil men for doing nothing wrong himself: "For, lo, they lie in wait for my soul: the mighty are gathered against me; not for my transgression, nor for

my sin, O Lord. They run and prepare themselves without my fault...
"(Psalm 59:3-4). When looked at without the enlightenment of God,
such testing can bring us perilously close to the place of falling of
which David spoke in the second verse of Psalm 73. After seeing
the truth, David repented, saying, "If I say, I will speak thus, behold,
I should offend against the generation of thy children," and "Thus
my heart was grieved, and I was pricked in my reins. So foolish was
I, and ignorant: I was as a beast before thee." (Psalm 73:15&21&22)
David acknowledges that his former thinking of enviousness for
the prosperity of the wicked was no better than the thinking of an
ignorant animal - unenlightened, foolish, and offensive. God's
caring efforts, working His great love toward His people through
His daily chastening, correcting, and helping (in the realm of things
eternal and invisible) would be counted as worthless by such base
thinking. David was deeply convicted of his error. He realized that
"whom the Lord loveth He chasteneth!" (Heb. 12:6).

Then, David summarizes wisely. Turning his eyes away from the
prosperity of others and fixing his gaze upon His Lord he writes:
"Nevertheless I am continually with thee: thou hast holden me by
my right hand. Thou shalt guide me with thy counsel, and afterward
receive me to glory. Whom have I in heaven but thee? And there is
none upon earth that I desire beside thee. My flesh and my heart
faileth: but God is the strength of my heart, and my portion forever.
For, lo, they that are far from thee shall perish: thou hast destroyed
all them that go a whoring from thee. But it is good for me to draw
near to God: I have put my trust in the Lord God, that I may declare
all thy works." (Psalm 73:23-28) We can say nothing else except God
is truly good to me, as we know and stand in the fact that we are
loved by Him, in every circumstance.

Finding Joy in Our Trials

Heavenly Father, thank You for your faithfulness. Your answer to prayer is amazing, as we see Your love and caring revealed toward us each day. Your word is a rock upon which we may stand and never fall. Your arms are outstretched to uphold us in each moment of trial and testing. Your power is manifest for our benefit and protection as we navigate the challenges of life with our eyes upon You. Give us patience, peace, and strength of faith, that we may glorify You in the face of adversity, challenge, and uncertainty. Lord, people's hearts shall fail them for the things that come to pass around us. May our hearts be strengthened to bring light and hope amid such darkness. In Jesus's name we pray. Amen.

That The Trial of Your Faith... May Be Found unto Praise
(1 Peter 1:7)

There are seasons to our walk and relationship with the Lord. Some are harsh, as the bitter cold of winter. Some are refreshing, as the warmth and fragrance of spring. At times, we feel the prolonged heat of summer, wishing for one cooler day. And the transition of fall is beautiful, though it signals the coming of yet another winter season. Peter speaks of being in a season of heaviness through manifold temptations. (1 Peter 1:6) This being a time of testing, as he further explains. Later, in 1 Peter 4:12, Peter speaks a caring reminder to the believer, saying "Beloved, think it not strange concerning the fiery trial, which is to try you, as though some strange thing happened unto you." This reminder needs to be spoken often, for we sometimes forget that the seasons change, and that we will most likely face many a winter season before the end of our journey. We may be fresh from the wonders of a spring, summer and fall in our walk with Jesus, but another winter will come our way.

There is a deepening work of transformation which the Holy Spirit seeks to accomplish in each heart cleansed by the blood of the Lamb and purchased of God. Faith is a precious thing which God seeks to refine and perfect as we come through many different experiences in this life. 1 Peter 1:5 reads: "Who are kept by the power of God through faith and salvation..." In all seasons, in all hardships, in all times of blessing, we are kept by the power of God, through faith, unto a purposed end planned by God-our salvation, our inheritance in eternity. We are kept by faith! During the testing, we are kept. We are not left alone. We are not abandoned to the strength of the circumstance or left to be crushed by the challenge. We are kept! Though the winds may seem to blow us off course and threaten our safety, yet we are kept and guided through each challenge as our faith is exercised to praise and trust the Lord.

Difficulties can cause us heaviness. We feel the reality of the pain of sickness, the worry of finances, the concern for loved ones, the anxiety of concern over many things which touch our lives. Faith doesn't necessarily take the heaviness away, but we will be kept through it, lifted above it, and shown the love and provisions of God as we place our trust in Him. We will be brought through it, into the planned blessings of God. We will not be left forsaken, even though we may feel that way at times. Some strange thing touching our lives may not be what we expected in our walk with Jesus, but to Him it is not strange, it is a tool of refining, a hand of divine love, seeking to make us more into the image of Jesus than we were before. "That the trial of your faith, being much more precious than of gold that perisheth, though it be tried with fire, might be found unto praise and honour and glory at the appearing of Jesus Christ." (1 Peter 1:7) It takes the fire of circumstances to prepare our hearts for the refining work of the Spirit of God. We must be softened by the heat to be molded by His hand. The impurities of our hearts are removed by His love as we seem to be melted by the heat of the trials. Just as gold is heated to be purified and shaped.

In the heat of God's transforming fire, claim that you indeed are kept by the power of God. Claim it amid the worst of circumstances. Stand in faith upon the promises of God's word. Take them as your own, for they are His gift to you. As we learn to see difficulty as His refining of our faith, then we gain great insight into the purposes of His work in our inner life and the outer circumstance loses its power to destroy. Yes, it may try us. Yes, it may feel heavy and dark. But it cannot destroy us, for we are kept by the power of God through faith.

We must not let the enemy destroy our faith. Peter admonishes us to "gird up the loins of your mind, be sober, and hope to the end." (1 Peter 1:13) Hope right on through the trials of faith; hope to the end. An absolute determination to trust Him is a clear manifestation of the finest purification of our faith. In Chapter four he continues, "forasmuch then as Christ hath suffered for us in the flesh, arm yourselves likewise with the same mind." (1 Peter 4:1) This mind set will help us to remember to not think it strange when we are tested.

Peter speaks in 1 Peter 1:6 of two distinctly opposite emotions taking place at the same time in our walk with Jesus - rejoicing and heaviness. This is healthy, for it depicts a soul that is rejoicing over the salvation of God and the nearness of the Holy Spirit, while at the same time being heavy over what is being experienced here on earth to accomplish God's deeper work in our hearts. This is the proper perspective which will enable us to come through the testing refined and strengthened, not destroyed. It is an attitude of faith which proclaims, I am focused upon and have accepted as mine, the great promise of God's love and eternal salvation through Jesus Christ. Come what may on my journey to eternity, I will rejoice in that promise. I will rejoice in His presence with me each day, though I suffer through many trials for the time being. I rejoice, for in all things, and through all things, I am kept by the power and love of God. This is the refining of faith which will be found to glorify the Lord at His coming!

Learn To Stand Amid Unbelieving Opinions

Heavenly Father, we come to You to be touched by the life-changing power only You possess. We cannot make ourselves better in Your sight. The mere exercising of diligence in the skills and gifts given does not mean we have grown thereby. The successes we may experience in the world do not always equate to growth in the Spirit. All the experiences we pass through will only help to make us into Your likeness if we yield and learn the precious lessons You have placed in them. Help us discover the treasures you desire us to find in the many differing settings of our lives. Let our focus be on those things of eternal value and grant us wisdom to know where to place our priorities. At the end of the day, may we look up to see that we have yielded to Your gentle promptings, shunned the temptations to yield to the flesh, yielded to be a good witness in our actions and words, and left behind some fragrance of Your gracious presence. In Jesus's name we pray, Amen.

They Agreed Not Among Themselves (Acts 28:25)

Upon Paul's arrival in Rome as a prisoner he called the chief Jews together to speak with them about his captivity and why he had appealed to Caesar. As he spoke to them, they said that no letters had been sent to them regarding Paul, nor had any of the brethren spoken anything about him. They did acknowledge they had heard about Paul's sect, and they understood it to be evil spoken of everywhere. They went on to say they wanted to hear what Paul had to say about his beliefs. They were curious, intrigued, or even perhaps genuinely interested to learn of the preaching of Jesus. Following this first meeting with Paul, the Jewish leaders arranged a day for Paul to speak to them. (Acts 28:16-23)

Upon the appointed day, a good number of people came to Paul's place of residence to hear him speak. All day long, Paul spoke to them about Jesus and demonstrated from scripture how Jesus was the Christ. He gave them clear examples from the law of Moses and the writings of the prophets. At the end of the day, we are told in verse 24, "and some believed the things which were spoken, and some believed not." (Acts 28:24) The preaching of the Gospel will more times than not have a similar result, some will believe, and some will not. What happened next is where every soul needs to exercise caution. The good received from the word of God can be destroyed quickly if we are not prepared for this likely subsequent event. Discussion! Discussion with the hope of reaching agreement with others, or support for our position from others.

Following Paul's teaching of the message of Jesus as Savior, we are told that some believed, and some believed not. Then we read, "When they agreed not among themselves, they departed." (Acts 28:25) A time of discussion took place between those who believed and those who did not. Doubt and unbelief were poured over the hearts of those who did believe from the mouths of those who did not. The resistance of the non-believers seemed to carry the day, for Paul's closing words to the entire group were, "Well spake the Holy Ghost by Esaias the prophet unto our fathers, saying, go unto this people, and say, hearing ye shall hear, and shall not understand; and seeing ye shall see, and not perceive: For the heart of this people is waxed gross, and their ears are dull of hearing, and their eyes have they closed; lest they should be converted, and I should heal them. Be it known therefore unto you, that the salvation of God is sent unto the Gentiles, and that they will hear it." (Acts 28:25-28 selected passages)

We then read, after Paul had spoken these last words of rebuke, "The Jews departed, and had great reasoning among themselves." (Acts 28:29) What is to be learned from this passage of scripture? Simply, reason not with others about what God is speaking to your own heart. Take your questions and reasoning to God Himself. Search out the scriptures for yourself and trust God to clarify any confusion through prayer and patient waiting upon Him. Do not seek to find support among friends and family. They may not be open to the things of God. The Spirit works on each heart individually. If many are touched, it is because they were individually ministered to by God. Those who receive not the things of the Spirit cannot be looked to for consensus. The group of Jews in Acts 28 left the gathering in disagreement and in a state of great reasoning. They did not leave standing firmly upon the truth that was shared by Paul.

In Matthew 13, Jesus gives us the parable of the Sower. In this parable we see several different results upon the hearts of those who heard the word of God. In verses 19-23 we see that some people hear the word and do not understand it. The wicked one then comes and takes away that which was sown. The result is the word is not received, nor believed. Others hear and believe for a while, but when difficulty comes because of their belief they abandon their faith. Others believe yet become too involved in other desires and are unfruitful in their lives. Yet others hear the word and believe and continue in their faith. If you were to put together a group of people from each category described in the parable, it is highly doubtful you could reach a consensus of agreement among them. Those who did not understand the word would cast a shadow over the faith of the others. Those who had abandoned their faith would likely seek to justify their position. Those who were new in their faith could be affected by the unbelief of the others. The result would probably be similar to what Paul observed among the Jews in Acts 28. To be in a state of great reasoning and disagreement is not profitable for the soul.

We need to be aware of this trap and seek to work out our own salvation with the Savior, not with the others in our lives. Has God quickened His truth to your heart? Then trust in that work of the Spirit and seek to grow through study of the word and prayer.

Do not be discouraged if others don't share what God has shown you. Keep them in your prayers, but do not let unbelief quench the work of the Spirit in your own heart, regardless of the source of the opposition.

Cutting The Ropes
of Self Confidence

Heavenly Father, help us to trust You more. Cause us to understand the benefit of releasing all things into Your control. Our efforts are ineffective and feeble by comparison to Yours. That which we would manipulate for our benefit would be a greater blessing if left to You. You have our best at heart. Thank You and praise You for Your great care toward us. The thoughts You think toward us are thoughts of goodness and blessing. It isa good thing to learn of our own helplessness, for then we look more to You and rely more upon Your mercy and love. Teach us Your ways, that we may walk in the light of Your understanding in each of our daily challenges. In Jesus's name we pray. Amen.

Cut Off the Ropes... Let Her Fall Away (Acts 27 :32)

Paul, after serving the Lord for many years, was taken prisoner and was being sent to Rome because he had appealed to Caesar following the Jews' accusations against him. Aboard a ship in the custody of a centurion named Julius, Paul found himself completely in the control of others. He had no say on when and where the ship would sail. Although he had admonished them not to risk the ship, for he perceived the sailing to be dangerous. (Acts 27:9-11) His advice was rejected, and Paul was compelled to sail into a fate he perceived to be hazardous. He had no choice.

Shortly thereafter, the ship encountered a severe storm. In Acts 27:18-20 we read: "And we being exceedingly tossed with a tempest, the next day they lightened the ship; and the third day we cast out with our own hands the tackling of the ship. And when neither sun nor stars in many days appeared, and no small tempest lay on us, all hope that we should be saved was then taken away." Paul, having warned them not to sail, being a prisoner with no options, captive against his will, was with them in this dire. situation. And so was the Lord! Paul stood and spoke to all aboard, "Sirs, ye should have hearkened unto me, and not have loosed from Crete, and to have gained this harm and loss. And now I exhort you to be of good cheer: for there shall be no loss of any man's life among you, but of the ship. For there stood by me this night the angel of God, whose I am, and whom I serve, saying, Fear not, Paul; thou must be brought before Caesar: and, lo, God hath given thee all them that sail with thee. Wherefore, sirs, be of good cheer: for I believe God, that it shall be even as it was told me. Howbeit we must be cast upon a certain island." (Acts 27:21-26)

In appearance, Paul was the captive being taken on this journey by the centurion and in the control of the captain of the ship. In God's eyes, all the others were sailing with Paul, for the angel of God said to him, "God hath given thee all them that sail with thee." (Acts 27:24) God was keeping Paul and granting protection to all around him, even though they did not heed sound advice and were most probably ignorant of the Lord. Nothing is capable of separating us from the love and protection of the Lord! Certainly, circumstances beyond our control are well within the control of God!

As the ship, after fourteen nights at sea, began to approach land, the crew set anchors, fearing they would hit rocks in the dark of the night if they ventured too close to shore. (Acts 27:27-29.) Then, seeking to save themselves, the crew attempted to flee the main ship in the smaller boat on board. Paul warned that if the crew left, the rest aboard, including the soldiers, could not be saved. At this warning, the soldiers cut the ropes and let the boat fall away into the stormy sea. There was now no means of escape from the ship. All would share in the fate which lay ahead. This last little boat could well have represented the last possible way for any of the men to save themselves. They now were cast upon the mercies of God alone, with no other options. Frankly, this is not a bad place to be! I wonder how often we seek to escape a situation by lowering our lifeboat into the sea for fear of what may come. Perhaps a better approach is to "cut off the ropes of the boat and let her fall off." (Acts 27:32) To have nothing of ourselves left to rely upon, and wait patiently upon the Lord, is a sure place of peace and ultimate victory.

Having no way of escape, Paul spoke to the men to encourage them to eat, and again promised that "there shall not a hair fall from the head of any of you." (Acts 27:34) They then waited for the light of day to try to sail closer to land. The ship ran aground and began to be broken in pieces, so into the sea went every soul. Those who could swim did so, and those who could not held onto pieces of the ship to float. We then read in Acts 27:44, "And so it came to pass, that they escaped all safe to land."

As the events unfolded, there were times of uncertainty and hopelessness. Lives were threatened. Just before leaping into the sea to swim for land, the soldiers wanted to kill the prisoners, including Paul. God intervened and caused the centurion to keep the soldiers from killing the prisoners, for he wished to save Paul. At each step, God spoke to Paul to comfort him and help in the situation or moved others to accomplish His purposes. This was a rough journey. Fourteen days at sea in a severe storm, the loss of the ship, and the threatened loss of life. The beauty of the story is the faithfulness of God to His people regardless of the journey! Blessing and provision do not always come in a package of serenity and calm. Here, amid a storm, we find God dispensing hope, guidance, encouragement, and ultimately deliverance from the danger. It was messy, difficult, and stressful, but it was a journey He was aware of and one He took with Paul. He will take our difficult journeys with us also.

Safety In the Midst of Danger

Heavenly Father, we thank You that You will finish the good work You have begun within us. It is Your work, Lord, and we are grateful as You continue to minister to us by giving us more understanding into Your ways. Your word is full of more treasures than a lifetime can discover. Thank You for the Holy Spirit who comes to help us as we seek You. Continue to give us greater light in those areas where we do not see clearly. Quicken to us the truth which strengthens us in challenging situations, brings us joy in all things, and brings us peace as we rest in Your care. Forgive us for our ignorance and lack of faith. Mold us into Your own image Lord, by the inner work of Your Spirit. In Jesus's name we pray. Amen.

But He, Passing Through the Midst of Them Went His Way
(Luke 4:30)

Following the temptations of the Lord described in Luke 4:1-13, Jesus "returned in the power of the Spirit into Galilee: and there went out a fame of him through all the region round about. And he taught in their synagogues, being glorified of all." (Luke 4: 14-15) Jesus began to be received of many as He taught and ministered to the people. The Holy Spirit's anointing rested upon Him. As He taught, people were deeply touched, so much so that His fame spread throughout the region. Then we read that He came to Nazareth, the area where He had been raised. Here he proceeded into the synagogue, as He was accustomed to doing, and stood up to read. He read, "The Spirit of the Lord is upon me, because he hath anointed me to preach the gospel to the poor; he hath sent me to heal the brokenhearted, and to preach deliverance to the captives, and recovering of sight to the blind, to set at liberty them that are bruised, to preach the acceptable year of the Lord." (Luke 4:18-19) As He sat down, every eye was upon Him. The way He had spoken, quickened by the Spirit, had caught their attention. He told them, "This day is this scripture fulfilled in your ears." (Luke 4:21) And we read that "All bear him witness and wondered at the gracious words which proceeded out of his mouth." (Luke 4:22) But then we read of their doubt and confusion as they asked one another, "Is not this Joseph's son?" (Luke 4:22)

Though they bore witness in their hearts, their minds and unbelief blinded them to His ministry. They saw only Joseph's son, not the Son of God. Jesus then gave them two examples from the scriptures of when God chose not to minister to the people of Israel, but rather to foreigners. The comparison was made to demonstrate that in times past, unbelief had prevented God's children from receiving God's blessing, guidance, and correction through God's prophets. The same unbelief that was now preventing them from receiving what Jesus would give them. Jesus told the story of the widow woman who lived in Sidon, and had been fed by the Lord as she provided shelter for Elijah. God sent Elijah there for his protection and provision rather than to any widow in Israel. At the time, Israel was under the rule of King Ahab, a man who had turned his back on God and caused Israel to sin greatly. Elijah had foretold of a drought, which brought hard times to Israel, and Ahab sought after Elijah, blaming him for the drought and Israel's troubles. God chose to send Elijah to this *foreigner's* home to provide for him, as well as the widow.

Next, Jesus told of the healing of Naaman, a Syrian in the days of Elisha. Jesus explained that there were many lepers in Israel at this time, but none had been healed, only Naaman, and he was a Syrian. The king of Israel thought that Naaman's request for healing was a provocation, so strange was it to his ears. Elijah said, "Send him to me and he shall know there is a prophet in Israel." (2 Kings 5:8) From these examples we could conclude that Jesus was showing them that the power of God had been present in those times, but Israel had not sought God to be healed, or to be helped in the famine. Or their hearts were not right, and thus they were prevented from receiving His help and blessing. God was present to heal Naaman, who came to Israel seeking to be healed. God provided for the widow woman and Elijah during the famine, and God healed her son when he became sick. (1 Kings 17) Jesus infers that Elijah and Elisha were not honored in their own country, and that God blessed those who did receive them, though they were not Jews. "Verily I say unto you, no prophet is accepted in his own country." (Luke 4:24) Jesus was revealing their unbelief to them, using these past examples, and they resented Him for doing so.

Upon hearing Jesus's words, the people in the synagogue in Nazareth, "were filled with wrath, and rose up, and thrust him out of the city, and led him unto the brow of the hill whereon their city was built, that they might cast him down headlong." (Luke 4:28-29) They were greatly offended by the words of Jesus. He had accused them of not honoring God's prophets. He had said that by not receiving His words they were rejecting God's messenger. They refused to accept that. They were correct in their own eyes, and Joseph's son was not going to reprimand them. Unbelief and hardness of heart prevented them from receiving God's blessing through Jesus.

An angry crowd dragged the Lord out of the synagogue and out to the edge of the hill on which their city was built. They intended to throw Him down headfirst. This was a violent crowd, and the Lord was being swept away with their anger and malice. They had taken hold of Him and dragged Him to within moments of being cast down the hill. Then we read: "But he, passing through the midst of them went his way." (Luke 4:30) Somehow, God caused this mob to lose control of Jesus. He did not lift Jesus out of the angry crowd. He did not sweep Him away in the Spirit. Simply, God caused Jesus to be free from their ill intentions, and so He walked "through the midst of them." (Luke 4:30) This is a beautiful message! Right in the middle of a very adverse experience, God made a way for Jesus to go His way! The might of the crowd was powerless. A path was made right through the adversity, not by being removed from it.

There is no adversity, challenge, or difficulty through which the Lord will not make a way for those whose eyes and faith are focused upon Him. The surrounding difficulty may not change, but through it God will make a way! There is no power capable of keeping us from going His way as our faith is placed in Him. There may be times when we come close to the edge of the hill of destruction, but we can believe God to make a way even then! Elijah was safe in the widow's home and was fed in the midst of the famine. Jesus was safe amid the angry crowd. We are in His hands *always,* without exception, and in this we can rejoice.

The Hazards of Pride

Heavenly Father, we bow before You, for You alone are worthy of our praise and adoration. We cannot count the ways You have helped us. We are amazed at Your attentiveness to our prayers and needs. You do not need to be so merciful and caring toward us, for we have done nothing to deserve Your love, yet You love us. For this we are grateful. Grant that we may never turn from seeking Your face, Lord, especially in times of blessing and rest. Testing has a way of throwing us into Your arms, while times of rest tend to find us lazy. Kindle a fresh fire of desire to seek You, and to yield to Your purposes in our lives. In Jesus's name we pray. Amen.

His Heart Was Lifted Up: Therefore, There Was Wrath Upon Him

(2 Chronicles 32:25)

It is difficult to walk in the blessings of the Lord. Difficult because it is easy for us to fall into thinking too highly of ourselves. Some of the greatest kings of Israel fell from a godly heart attitude after years of dedication to God. Three of them were Solomon, Josiah, and Hezekiah. They started their rule humble and broken before the Lord, served Him without compromise, only to later fall into difficulty. While the reasons vary, the fact remains: even the greatest of God's servants may fall if their heart attitude ceases to be broken and contrite. We must never lose sight of our deep need for God's help, even after years of receiving His assistance.

Hezekiah's story is amazing. His strength and commitment to God were exceptional. In 2 Kings 18-20 and 2 Chronicles 29-32, we read of Hezekiah's life. Early in his reign, he sought to destroy all the things which hindered Judah from following the Lord. He even destroyed the brass serpent which Moses had made. For years, the children of Israel had burned incense unto it. No king before him had even recognized the idolatry in this. Hezekiah did! (2 Kings 18:4).

Following years of rule by an evil king, Hezekiah repaired the house of the Lord. Upon reopening it and establishing the order of sacrifice and offering, he wrote letters to all Israel for them to come to Jerusalem to keep the Passover unto the Lord. While he was laughed to scorn by most, many came and were blessed as they again followed the commandment of God. (2 Chron. 30:10) "So, there was great joy in Jerusalem." (2 Chron. 30:26) After this, there was a cleansing of the land as the people went out and "break the images in pieces, and cut down the groves, and threw down the high places and the altars." (2 Chron. 31:1) In all that Hezekiah did, he set his heart to please God, "and in every work that he began in the service of the house of God, and in the law, and in the commandments, to seek his God, he did it with his heart, and prospered." (2 Chron. 31:21)

Following his good works for God, Hezekiah faced a severe challenge. [*Commitment and dedication* spare none *of us from the testing and refining hand of* God.] The king of Assyria came to fight against Jerusalem. Hezekiah's faith was tested as the enemy shouted accusations against God and Hezekiah to all who could hear them on the walls of Jerusalem. Threatening letters were also sent. In this hour of despair, Hezekiah, and Isaiah the prophet, prayed and cried out to the Lord. At the hearing of the threat, we are told that Hezekiah, "went into the house of the Lord." (2 Kings 19:14)

Upon receiving the letter, he also, "went up into the house of the Lord, and spread it before the Lord." (2 Kings 19:14) It was this constant reliance upon God that prospered Hezekiah, even in the face of destruction. God answered the prayers of Hezekiah and Isaiah and sent an angel to destroy the leaders of the enemy army (2 Chron. 32:1-22). After these events, many began to greatly look up to Hezekiah. We read, "…and many brought gifts unto the Lord to Jerusalem and presents to Hezekiah king of Judah: so that he was magnified in the sight of all nations from thenceforth." (2 Chron. 32:23) Perhaps this was the beginning of Hezekiah's difficulty. Being praised by others can cause the heart to rise from its knees, ceasing to be humble and contrite.

In 2 Kings chapter 20, we read of the healing of Hezekiah, and God's miraculous sign to him to assure him of his healing. The sun moved backward ten degrees in the middle of the day! It was after this healing, that Hezekiah responded unwisely to letters from the prince of Babylon, who had written, "to enquire of the wonder that was done in the land." (Chron.32:31) We are told that "God left him, (Hezekiah) to try him, that he might know all that was in his heart." (2 Chron. 32:31) Hezekiah proceeded to receive the Babylonian visitors and show them the wonders of his treasures. (2 Kings 20:13) He boasted of his blessings, which were the gifts of God, and showed them off to the rulers of Babylon. Hezekiah did not respond well to the praises and acknowledgement he received from the prince of Babylon. He bowed to it, and his heart was lifted improperly in the sight of God. Isaiah was then sent to reprove Hezekiah (2 Kings 20:14-19). Two Chron. 32:25 summarizes: "But Hezekiah rendered not again according to the benefit done unto him; for his heart was lifted up: therefore, there was wrath upon him, and upon Judah and Jerusalem."

We rejoice, when on our knees we humble ourselves, beseech God and find His help. We need to exercise caution when we are praised of others, even for God's blessings. It can too easily lead to wrong actions and reproof from God if our hearts are lifted up. Jesus did not submit Himself to the praises of man, for we read: "Now when he was in Jerusalem at the Passover, in the feast day, many believed in his name, when they saw the miracles which he did. But Jesus did not commit himself unto them, because he knew all men, and needed not that any should testify of man: for he knew what was in man." (John 2:23-25) Care is constantly required to give God *all* of the praise and glory!

Hezekiah was first dedicated. Then his faith was tried, and he was humbled by the testing of an enemy invasion. Then he was lifted in his own eyes by his victory and healing. And finally, again, he was humbled by the words of Isaiah. (2 Chron. 32:26) The lifting up came with the victory and healing. Humility came with reproof and testing. Testing, trials, and reproof can all yield the desired result - humility - if we yield our hearts to Him. Caution must be exercised in the times of blessing and victory, lest we be lifted in our own eyes, and stumble as did Hezekiah!

Avoid Unnecessary Trouble

Heavenly Father, we rejoice in Your wonderful works. Barriers formed by wrong thinking, roots of sin which cause great difficulty, and our inability to see the source of the devastation, are healed, released, and corrected in the blink of an eye as Your Spirit ministers to our hearts to set us free. We pray for Your continued help in keeping us from the sin and trouble caused by our resistance. Grant us grace to release those things, and relationships, we are not meant to control. For by refusing to do so, we hinder our relationship with You and others. Hasten Your good work in us Lord, for as we look back upon past enlightenments, we desire to be helped in the areas we do not yet understand. It is Your great love which seeks to liberate us fully from the chains of sin which bind our hearts with wrong attitudes and thinking. We admit our great ignorance. We ask for Your continued help. In Jesus's name we pray. Amen.

Wherefore Let Him That Thinketh He Standeth Take Heed Lest He Fall (1 Cor. 10:12)

In the tenth chapter of 1 Corinthians, we are told an important fact concerning our reading and learning from the Old Testament writings. We read: "Now all these things happened unto them for examples: and they are written for our admonition. " (1 Cor. 10:11) We can learn from the triumphs and mistakes of those who have gone before us. Our understanding is enriched as we ponder the matters discussed and observe the actions of the people and the response of God. Today, our battles may not be in mortal combat and the kingdom we seek to protect may not be a vast land. More likely our battles are matters which touch our personal lives relating to family, work, ministry, and ourselves. The kingdom we seek to protect is a right heart attitude. It is the stance in the heart that is central in the stories of the Old Testament. While the scene of the events may be quite different than that of our personal lives, yet the lessons to be learned are the same.

In 2 Chronicles: 34 and 35, we read of the life of King Josiah. He was only eight years old when he began to reign. We are told: "And he did that which was right in the sight of the Lord, and walked in the ways of David his father, and declined neither to the right hand, nor to the left." (2 Chron. 34:2) When he was twenty-six, he committed to repair the house of the Lord. In the process, the book of the law of the Lord, given by Moses was found. As it was read to the king, he realized great wrath was promised to come upon the people because of their sins and their turning away from the Lord. Josiah set his heart to seek the Lord and sent a delegation to inquire of Huldah, the prophetess. We read: "And Hilkiah, and they that the king had appointed, went to Huldah the prophetess, the wife of Shallum the son of Tikvath, the son of Hasrah, keeper of the wardrobe;... and she answered them, Thus saith the Lord God of Israel, Tell ye the man that sent you to me, Thus saith the Lord, Behold, I will bring evil upon this place, and upon the inhabitants thereof, even all the curses that are written in the book which they have read before the king of Judah: because they have forsaken me, and have burned incense unto other gods, that they might provoke me to anger with all the works of their hands; therefore my wrath shall be poured out upon this place, and shall not be quenched. And as for the king of Judah, who sent you to enquire of the Lord, so shall ye say unto him, thus saith the Lord God of Israel concerning the words which thou hast heard; because thine heart was tender, and thou didst humble thyself before God, when thou heardest his words against this place, and against the inhabitants thereof, and humbledst thyself before me, and didst rend thy clothes, and weep before me; I have even heard thee also, saith the Lord. Behold, I will gather thee to thy fathers, and thou shalt be gathered to thy grave in peace, neither shall thine eyes see all the evil that I will bring upon this place, and upon the inhabitants of the same." (2 Chron. 34:22-28) God was moved to assist this young king because of his humble and sincere heart attitude.

Josiah continued to follow the Lord, as we read: "And Josiah took away all the abominations out of all the countries that pertained to the children of Israel, and made all that were present in Israel to serve, even to serve the Lord their God. And all his days they departed not from following the Lord, the God of their fathers." (2 Chron. 34:33) They also observed the Passover feast at Josiah's direction. It was said that there was no such Passover kept since the days of Samuel the prophet. (2 Chron. 35:18)

Josiah was a man whose heart was set to follow God. As a result, many turned their hearts to the Lord during Josiah's life. After the wonderful and correct things which Josiah had done, and the tremendous zeal he had for the Lord, the king of Egypt came up to fight against Charchemish, by the Euphrates. He did not come to fight with Josiah nor Judah. Nevertheless, Josiah decided to go and fight against the king of Egypt. Necho, king of Egypt, sent ambassadors to Josiah saying, "What have I to do with thee, thou king of Judah? I come not against thee this day, but against the house wherewith I have war: for God commanded me to make haste: forbear thee from meddling with God, who is with me, that he destroy thee not. Nevertheless, Josiah would not turn his face from him, but disguised himself, that he might fight with him, and hearkened not unto the words of Necho from the mouth of God and came to fight in the valley of Megiddo." (2 Chron. 35:20-22)

Josiah did not seek the counsel of God over this matter. He was stubborn in his insistence to fight the king of Egypt. Although concerned enough to disguise himself in the battle, his hiding did not protect him. As a result, he lost his life in the battle at a very young age. We read: "And the archers shot at king Josiah; and the king said to his servants, have me away; for I am sore wounded ... and they brought him to Jerusalem, and he died." (2 Chron. 35:23-24) We also will find no protection behind a disguise of our heart's deepest motives. God looks beneath our best disguises, to heal us of any wrong underlying motive. Where there is destruction, there is likely an insistence upon our own will. As we ponder the admonition in 1 Corinthians 10:12, we see the value of such advice: "let him that thinketh he standeth take heed lest he fall." All the good we may have done in the past will not keep us from the consequences of a wrong heart attitude today. If we take upon ourselves a thinking which does not rely upon the Lord in every moment for guidance and protection, we are vulnerable to defeat and difficulty. God helped Josiah when his heart was "tender, and he humbled himself before God." (2 Chron. 34:27) When his heart was lifted in a battle God did not want him to fight, God left him to his own destruction. [2 Chron. 35:22 discloses that the admonition for Josiah not to fight was from the mouth of God.]

May the Lord help us not take into our own pride His acts of mercy, help, victory, provision, and protection. Humble and *tender* is where our hearts will find the power and blessing of God.

Printed in the United States
by Baker & Taylor Publisher Services